My Job Sucks

Richard Lowe

The Writing King

My Job Sucks

Copyright © 2026 by Richard G. Lowe

Although every precaution has been taken to verify the accuracy of the information contained herein, the author and publisher assume no responsibility for any errors or omissions. No liability is assumed for damages that may result from the use of information contained within.

Trademarked names appear throughout this book. Rather than use a trademark symbol with every occurrence of a trademarked name, names are used in an editorial fashion, with no intention of infringement of the respective owner's trademark.

Table of Contents

See books by Richard Lowe at

https://masterofworlds.com

Get free publishing insights and industry updates at

https://thewritingking.substack.com

For ghostwriting and book coaching services see

https://thewritingking.com

Introduction: Welcome to the New Reality

Let me tell you something that's going to piss you off: you've been lied to your entire working life.

Every piece of career advice you've ever received, every motivational poster hanging in your office, every HR presentation about "company values" has been carefully crafted bullshit designed to keep you compliant, grateful, and most importantly, afraid.

The Fear They Want You to Feel

Right now, as you're reading this, you're probably carrying a knot of anxiety in your stomach about your job. Maybe it's the constant worry that you're one bad quarterly report away from a layoff. Maybe it's the sick feeling you get every time your boss calls an "impromptu meeting." Maybe it's the way you check your work email at 11 PM because you're terrified of missing something "urgent."

That fear isn't accidental. Companies have discovered that scared employees are productive employees. Scared employees don't ask for raises. Scared employees don't push back on unreasonable demands. Scared employees say "thank you" when they're asked to work weekends for the third month in a row.

You've been trained to think: "I'm lucky to have any job in this economy." "At least they're not laying people off." "I should be grateful they picked me." "What if I can't find anything else?"

The Truth That Sets You Free

Here's what they don't want you to realize: you have more power than they've led you to believe. Every single day, you wake up and choose to give them eight or more hours of your life. Every day, you bring skills, experience, and energy that create value for their business. Every day, you solve problems, handle crises, and keep their operation running.

You're not lucky to have a job. They're lucky to have you.

The moment you truly understand this, everything changes. The anxiety starts to fade. The desperation disappears. You stop making decisions from fear and start making them from strategic thinking.

How We Got Here

The old social contract between employers and employees died sometime around 2008, but nobody bothered to tell us. For decades, the deal was simple: work hard, be loyal, and the company will take care of you. Pensions, job security, predictable advancement. It was all real, once.

Then the world changed. Shareholders became more important than stakeholders. Quarterly profits became more important than long-term sustainability. Employees became "human resources," literally resources to be optimized, utilized, and discarded when no longer needed.

The pandemic and the AI revolution just made obvious what was already true: corporations view you as a cost center to be minimized, not a human being to be valued. When ChatGPT can write code and robots can flip burgers, all that talk about "family" and "loyalty" evaporates faster than free donuts in the break room.

Your Transformation Journey

This book exists for one reason: to give you the tools corporations desperately hope you never discover. Every chapter is designed to shift power back to you, to move you from reactive victim to strategic player.

We're going to start by understanding exactly what you're dealing with. You'll learn what you really want from work (and why those desires are completely reasonable), what corporations want from you (spoiler: it's not what they claim), and how the gig economy has created a third option that's neither freedom nor security.

Then we'll dive into tactical survival skills. You'll learn to spot toxic workplaces before you get trapped in them. You'll discover how to survive the disposable workforce mentality, game the work-life balance illusion, and deal with sociopathic bosses and toxic colleagues. You'll understand why your coworkers aren't your friends and why HR is definitely not your friend.

Most importantly, you'll learn why you stay in jobs you hate (hint: it's usually fear-based thinking that's been deliberately cultivated), and how to break free from that psychological prison.

The later sections focus on building your future: developing exit strategies, playing the corporate game without losing your soul, creating alternative income streams, and protecting your mental health in environments designed to destroy it.

Your Power Starts Here

By the time you finish this book, you'll never again lie awake at night worrying about job security. Not because you'll have found the perfect job (perfect jobs don't exist), but because you'll have built something better than security. You'll have built control.

You'll understand how to read the warning signs of layoffs before they happen. You'll know how to document everything to protect yourself legally. You'll have multiple income streams and skills that transfer across industries. You'll have an emergency fund that gives you the freedom to walk away from toxic situations.

Most importantly, you'll have shifted your mindset from "What if I lose my job?" to "What's my next chess move?"

This isn't about becoming cynical or bitter. It's about becoming strategic and empowered. It's about recognizing that the employment relationship is transactional, and making sure you're getting the better end of the transaction.

The Game Has Changed

The AI revolution, remote work, and the death of traditional career paths have created a new landscape. The old rules don't apply anymore. Company loyalty is dead. Job security is an illusion. The social safety net is full of holes.

But here's the thing: once you stop expecting the system to take care of you, you can start taking care of yourself. And you can do it better than any corporation ever could.

Welcome to your new reality. It's scarier than the old one, but it's also more honest. And in that honesty, you'll find your freedom.

Let's get started.

The Perfect Job (From Your Perspective)

"The only way to do great work is to love what you do. If you haven't found it yet, keep looking. Don't settle." - Steve Jobs

---

The Problem

You know what you want from work. Deep down, beneath all the corporate conditioning and "be grateful you have a job" messaging, you know exactly what would make you excited to get up on Monday morning. The problem is that admitting what you want feels dangerous, almost ungrateful. After years of being told to lower your expectations, you've started to believe that wanting fulfillment from your job is naive.

Here's the truth: your desires aren't unrealistic. They're not entitled millennial nonsense or fantasy thinking. What you want from work is completely reasonable, achievable, and frankly, what every human being deserves in exchange for eight hours of their finite life every day.

The real problem isn't your expectations. The real problem is that you've been convinced to settle for scraps while pretending to be grateful for the privilege.

Discussion

Let me tell you about five different people, each representing a different approach to work. Maybe you'll recognize yourself in one of them, or maybe you're a combination. Either way, their desires are completely reasonable, and understanding them is the first step toward getting what you want.

Meet Sarah. She's been at the same company for three years and has had four managers, none of whom could explain what she actually does. She spends her days making other people's bad ideas presentable. Last month she solved a problem in two hours that had been on the roadmap for six months. Nobody noticed. She's not asking to be CEO. She wants work that requires her actual brain, recognition that goes beyond "great job in the meeting today," and the autonomy to solve problems her way instead of the approved way.

Then there's Marcus. He has a spreadsheet on his home computer that tracks every layoff announcement in his industry going back four years. He updates it every Friday. He's survived three rounds of cuts at his current company, watched people with more tenure and better performance reviews get walked out with a box of desk stuff, and still can't sleep on Sunday nights. He's not asking for a guarantee. He's asking for a reasonable connection between doing good work consistently and still having a job next year.

Priya missed her daughter's recital for a 6 PM call that turned out to be optional. The person who organized it wasn't even on for the first fifteen minutes. She makes it to maybe half the things that matter. She's tried explaining this to three different managers. All three told her they supported work-life balance and then scheduled her for something that conflicted with a family obligation within two weeks. She's not lazy. She just wants to leave at 5:30 without the guilt trip.

David spent eight months building a system that saved his department forty hours a week. He got a $2,000 bonus. His VP got a performance multiplier that year. David's still doing the math. He wants to work somewhere the upside isn't completely severed from the output. If he creates something worth real money, he wants to participate in that reality, not watch it flow upward while he gets a gift card and a handshake.

Finally, there's Elena. She's been the unofficial expert on her company's most critical platform for six years. When things break, they call her. When the vendor comes in for a meeting, they bring her. When she asked for a title that reflected this, she was told the band structure didn't support it. Three months later they hired a director from outside who now manages her and has never touched the system. Elena wants to be compensated and recognized like the expert she already is, not managed by someone who's still asking her how things work.

Notice what all five of them have in common? None of them are asking for something impossible. They want basic human dignity, fair compensation for the value they create, and the chance to use their capabilities fully.

The reason these desires feel unrealistic is that most modern workplaces are designed to prevent them from being fulfilled. Companies have discovered that frustrated, slightly desperate employees work harder and complain less than satisfied ones.

Solutions

The good news is that you can engineer many of these elements into almost any job if you're strategic about it. Stop asking permission and start creating the conditions you want.

If you're like Sarah, stop waiting for your boss to assign you interesting work. Create it yourself. Identify problems in your organization that align with your interests and propose solutions. Volunteer for cross-functional projects. Build things in your spare time that demonstrate your capabilities. Keep a running record of your impact. When you can show concrete results, you earn the right to demand more interesting challenges and the autonomy to pursue them.

If you're like Marcus, understand that security doesn't come from your employer anymore. It comes from your skills, your network, and your financial cushion. Make yourself expensive to replace by developing capabilities your organization needs but can't easily find elsewhere. Build relationships with people who can hire you if your current job disappears. Save aggressively so you can survive being unemployed for longer than most people. Real security is knowing you'll be fine regardless of what your current employer does.

If you're like Priya, remember that boundaries aren't given, they're enforced. Start small. Don't check email after a certain time. Don't respond to non-urgent messages on weekends. Be reliable during work hours and completely unreachable during your personal time. Most bosses will adapt to clear, consistent boundaries if you maintain them without apology or explanation.

If you're like David, find ways to tie your compensation to your results. Negotiate bonuses based on outcomes you can control. Ask for equity if you're at a startup. Create side projects that could eventually replace your day job. The goal is to gradually shift your income from trading time for money to creating value that pays you repeatedly.

If you're like Elena, become genuinely indispensable by being the only person who knows how to do something critical. Then make sure everyone knows you're the only person who knows how to do it. Speak at conferences. Write about your expertise. Build a reputation outside your company. When you're known as an expert externally, your internal value skyrockets.

Exercises

First, figure out what type you are. Write down what you want from work, not what you think you should want or what seems realistic. Be honest about what would make you excited about Monday morning.

Second, audit your current situation. How far is your current job from your ideal? What elements are completely missing? What elements exist but could be stronger?

Third, identify three changes you could make in the next six months to move closer to your ideal. Don't think about what your boss would approve of. Think about what you could create or negotiate or develop that would give you more of what you want.

Fourth, research companies and roles that might naturally provide what you're looking for. Not so you can immediately jump ship, but so you know what's possible and what you should be working toward.

Perfect jobs don't exist. Stop accepting less than you deserve and start creating conditions that work for you. Your current employer will either adapt or you'll find one who will.

Either way, you win.

The Perfect Employee (From Corporate's Perspective)

"Corporations have been enthroned and an era of corruption in high places will follow." - Abraham Lincoln

The Problem

You think you understand what your company wants from you because you've read the job description, sat through the orientation, and nodded along during performance reviews. But here's what nobody tells you: what they say they want and what they really want are two completely different things. The disconnect between their stated values and their real priorities explains why workplace relationships feel fundamentally exploitative and why traditional career advice fails so spectacularly.

Every company has multiple levels of management, each with their own agenda, and you're caught in the middle trying to please masters who want contradictory things from you. Understanding what each level wants gives you the power to navigate their expectations strategically instead of stumbling around hoping your hard work will be noticed and rewarded.

Discussion

Let me break down what each level of corporate hierarchy really wants from you, stripped of all the mission statement bullshit and team-building rhetoric.

The C-suite executives, the ones making the big decisions from their corner offices, want you to be completely disposable while producing maximum output at minimum cost. They want you to work like you own the company while being paid like you're lucky to be there. They want you to be passionate about the mission when it's convenient and understanding when they make cuts that affect your livelihood but not theirs. They want you to adapt instantly to new priorities, learn new skills on your own time, and never, ever ask for anything that might impact their bonus structure.

Most of all, they want you to shut up and execute. They don't want your input on strategy, your suggestions for improvement, or your concerns about sustainability. They want widgets produced, numbers hit, and problems solved without having to hear about the human cost. You're a line item on a spreadsheet, and the goal is to maximize your output while minimizing your expense.

Middle management wants something entirely different. They want you to be competent enough to make them look good but not so competent that you threaten their position. They want you to be loyal to them personally, not just to the company. They want you to make their life easier by handling things they don't want to deal with while giving them credit for your successes.

Your manager wants you to be the kind of employee who makes their job effortless. You anticipate problems before they become crises. You handle difficult conversations they don't want to have. You work late to meet impossible deadlines they promised to their boss without consulting you. And when things go well, you graciously allow them to take credit at the leadership meeting.

Most crucially, they want you to never make them look bad in front of their superiors. This means no surprises, no pushback on unrealistic timelines, and definitely no going around them when they're being incompetent or obstructive. Your success reflects well on them, but your problems become their problems, and they hate having problems.

HR, despite all their talk about employee engagement and workplace culture, has one primary goal: protect the company from you. They want you to be compliant, documentable, and lawsuit-proof. They want you to believe they're on your side while they gather evidence that could be used against you if needed. They want you to voluntarily give up rights you don't know you have and accept policies that benefit the company at your expense.

HR wants you to be the kind of employee who never files complaints, never questions policies, and never requires them to do anything that might create legal liability. They want you to handle harassment and discrimination quietly, accept inadequate compensation gracefully, and leave voluntarily if you become a problem instead of forcing them to fire you.

When HR talks about "cultural fit," they mean someone who won't rock the boat, won't ask uncomfortable questions, and won't create documentation that could be subpoenaed later. They want team players who play by rules designed to protect the company, not the team.

The shareholders and board members, the people who own the company, want you to generate maximum return on their investment while being invisible. They want your productivity to increase every quarter while your compensation stays flat. They want you to be grateful for cost-of-living adjustments that don't cover the cost of living. They want you to accept benefit cuts disguised as "improvements" and buy into company stock programs that benefit them more than you.

They want you to believe that company success will eventually trickle down to employee benefits, even though decades of evidence prove that's not how it works. They want you to feel invested in stock prices and quarterly results that determine their wealth while having no real influence over the decisions that drive those numbers.

Solutions

Now that you understand what each level really wants, you can appear to give them what they need while protecting your own interests and building your exit strategy.

For the C-suite, become the employee who delivers results without creating problems. Hit your numbers consistently.

Solve problems before they reach executive attention. But do all of this while tracking your contributions systematically and building skills that transfer to other companies. Make yourself valuable to them while making yourself valuable to their competitors.

When executives want passion and loyalty, give them performance and reliability instead. Passion fades, but consistent results build your reputation. When they want you to work like an owner, negotiate compensation that reflects ownership. When they want you to adapt to new priorities, make sure your adaptability is compensated and recognized.

For middle management, master the art of managing up. Make your boss look good, but make sure you get credit for your contributions. Handle the problems they don't want to deal with, but create documentation that shows your problem-solving capabilities. Meet their impossible deadlines, but track the cost of those unrealistic expectations.

Be the employee who makes their life easier while building evidence of your own competence. Take on high-visibility projects that showcase your abilities. Volunteer for cross-functional work that expands your network. And always, always have a paper trail that shows your contributions.

For HR, become impossible to build a case against. Follow policies precisely. Get everything in writing. Respond to requests promptly and professionally. But understand that every interaction with HR is potentially being evaluated for legal risk. Be friendly but not personal. Be helpful but not naive.

When HR wants compliance, give them professional compliance while protecting your rights. Know your state's employment laws. Understand your company's policies better than they do. And remember that anything you say to HR can and will be used to protect the company, not you.

Exercises

Start by mapping your company's power structure. Who really makes decisions about your work, your compensation, and your future? Who influences those decisions? Understanding the real hierarchy helps you focus your relationship-building efforts where they'll have the most impact.

Next, audit your current relationships with each level. Are you making the C-suite's life easier or harder? Are you helping your manager succeed or creating problems for them? Are you giving HR any reason to see you as a risk?

Then, identify ways you can appear to meet each level's needs while advancing your own agenda. How can you deliver the results executives want while building your personal brand? How can you support your manager's goals while expanding your own responsibilities? How can you stay compliant with HR while protecting your legal position?

Finally, create a strategy for each relationship that serves your long-term interests. You're not trying to become their ideal employee. You're trying to appear valuable enough to keep around while building capabilities that make you valuable elsewhere.

You're not trying to change what they want. You're trying to use what they want to get what you need. Play their game long enough to build the skills, experience, and financial cushion that gives you the freedom to play by your own rules.

The goal isn't to become the perfect employee. The goal is to appear perfect while preparing to become something better: someone with options.

The Gig Economy (And How to Use It)

"In the gig economy, the only job security is the security you create for yourself." - Reid Hoffman

The Problem

The gig economy was supposed to be the great liberation. Work when you want, be your own boss, unlimited earning potential, freedom from corporate bullshit. At least that's what the Silicon Valley marketing machine wants you to believe. The reality is that the gig economy has created a third category of work that combines the worst aspects of traditional employment with the worst aspects of entrepreneurship, wrapped in the shiny packaging of "flexibility."

You're not an employee, so you get no benefits, no job security, and no legal protections. But you're also not really your own boss because algorithms control your work, platforms set your rates, and you can be deactivated without explanation or appeal. You get all the risk and responsibility of self-employment with none of the control or upside of business ownership.

The gig economy isn't solving the fundamental problem of work. It's just shifting the exploitation model from time-based to outcome-based while making workers pay for their own equipment, insurance, and retirement.

Discussion

Let's start with what they promise you. Complete flexibility over your schedule. Work as much or as little as you want. Be your own boss. No commute, no office politics, no incompetent managers breathing down your neck. Set your own rates. Build your own client base. Live anywhere you want. Work in your pajamas.

It sounds amazing because it addresses every complaint people have about traditional employment. Tired of asking permission to take time off? Work whenever you want. Hate your boss? You don't have one. Sick of office drama? Work from home. Want to earn more? Just work more hours or charge higher rates.

The marketing is brilliant because it targets the exact pain points that make people miserable in regular jobs. The gig economy platforms position themselves as the antidote to corporate toxicity. They're not your employer, they're your partner. They're not exploiting you, they're empowering you.

Now let's talk about the reality. That flexibility comes with complete income uncertainty. You might make great money one month and barely cover your expenses the next. There's no predictable paycheck, no paid time off, no sick leave. If you don't work, you don't get paid. If you get sick, you're screwed. If the platform changes its algorithm or fee structure, your income can disappear overnight.

The "be your own boss" thing is laughable. You're not setting your own rates in most cases. The platform sets them, and you either accept what they offer or you don't work. You're not choosing your own clients. The algorithm chooses for you based on factors you can't control and often can't even see. You're not building your own business. You're building their business while they keep the valuable asset (the customer relationship) and you keep the labor.

You're responsible for all the costs of doing business, but you don't own any of the business. You pay for your car, your gas, your phone, your insurance, your equipment. You handle customer service issues. You deal with difficult clients. You absorb the cost of cancellations, no-shows, and non-payment. But the platform owns the technology, the brand, the customer data, and the relationship.

The platforms have figured out how to get all the benefits of having employees (people who do the work) without any of the costs or responsibilities of being an employer (benefits, job security, legal compliance). They've created a workforce that's even more disposable than traditional employees because they can be cut off instantly without severance, notice, or explanation.

But here's where it gets really insidious. The gig economy has trained traditional employers to adopt the same mentality. Why hire full-time employees when you can hire contractors? Why provide benefits when you can classify people as independent workers? Why offer job security when you can create a "flexible" workforce that expands and contracts based on demand?

The gig economy mindset is bleeding into regular employment. Companies are adopting gig-style metrics (constant performance monitoring), gig-style compensation (pay for results, not time), and gig-style job security (none). They want employees who think like entrepreneurs (taking personal responsibility for outcomes) while being treated like contractors (disposable and replaceable).

So now you have three options, and they all suck in different ways. Traditional employment gives you some security but no autonomy. Gig work gives you some autonomy but no security. And entrepreneurship gives you potential for both but requires capital, skills, and risk tolerance that most people don't have.

Solutions

Stop thinking about these as mutually exclusive choices and start thinking about how to use each one strategically to build the career you want.

The smart play is to treat gig work as a steppingstone, not a destination. Use it to build skills, test business ideas, and create income streams while you're building something better. Don't fall for the platform's marketing about being your own boss.

You're not. You're a subcontractor who can be fired at any time for any reason.

Start by using gig work to supplement your traditional income, not replace it. Keep your day job while you figure out what platforms work for you, what skills are in demand, and how much you can realistically earn. Use the gig income to build your emergency fund, pay down debt, or invest in developing more valuable skills.

Once you understand how the gig economy works, you can start building a portfolio of income sources that gives you both security and flexibility. Maybe you do consulting work in your area of expertise, drive for a rideshare company during peak hours, and sell products online. None of these alone provides enough income or security, but together they create a safety net that's more resilient than any single employer.

The goal is to gradually shift from trading time for money to creating value that pays you repeatedly. Use gig platforms to test business ideas with minimal risk. If you're thinking about starting a consulting practice, try freelancing on platforms first to see if there's demand for your services. If you want to start an e-commerce business, try selling on existing marketplaces before building your own website.

Most importantly, use gig work to build skills and relationships that transfer beyond the platforms. Don't just complete tasks, build expertise. Don't just serve clients, create relationships. Don't just earn money, build a reputation. The platform might own the transaction, but you own the knowledge and experience you gain from it.

Eventually, you want to graduate from being dependent on platforms to having your own direct relationships with clients or customers. Use the platforms to learn the business, understand the market, and build your capabilities. Then use that knowledge to create something you own and control.

Build your own website. WordPress, Wix, Squarespace — it doesn't take long to learn, and it gives you something no platform can take away. Your site is your real home base. The gig platforms and social media accounts are outposts you use to drive traffic back to it. Set it up so Google can find it. Post on social media as yourself, pointing back to your site, not just to your platform profile. Most gig platforms will actively prevent you from linking out — they want your reputation to live inside their walls, not yours. That's exactly why your site matters. It's the one thing in this arrangement you actually own.

Before you commit to any platform, run the numbers they won't run for you. Uber doesn't talk much about gas, wear on your car, depreciation, or what it costs to drive strangers around for hours. Airbnb skips the part about squatters, property damage, theft, and the insurance gaps you'll discover only after something goes wrong. None of them mention retirement or health coverage, because that's your problem now, not theirs. Add self-employment tax — 15.3% on top of income tax, money that never shows up in your platform payout — and the real hourly rate after all expenses can get ugly fast. Some gig work is genuinely worth it. Some of it is a slow loss that looks like income until April.

The hybrid approach works for traditional employment too. Instead of quitting your job to become a full-time freelancer, start freelancing on evenings and weekends while you build your client base. Instead of leaving your corporate job to start a business, start the business as a side project while you still have health insurance and a steady paycheck.

Exercises

First, audit your current skills to see what gig opportunities might be available to you. What can you do that people will pay for on a project basis? What knowledge do you have that others need? What services could you provide in your spare time?

Second, research the platforms and opportunities in your area or field. What are the real earning potentials? What are the costs and requirements? What are the reviews from people who have tried it? Don't rely on the platform's marketing materials. Find real people who are doing the work and ask them about their experience.

Third, test one or two gig opportunities while keeping your regular job. Start small. Invest minimal time and money until you understand how it works and whether it's viable for you. Track everything: hours worked, money earned, expenses incurred, taxes owed, wear and tear on equipment.

Fourth, use what you learn to develop a long-term strategy. Is this something you could scale up? Is there a way to build recurring income instead of constantly finding new gigs? Could you eventually cut out the platform and work directly with clients? How does this fit into your overall career and financial goals?

The gig economy isn't inherently good or bad. It's a tool. Use it to build something better instead of getting trapped in the cycle of constantly hustling for the next gig.

Don't let the platforms convince you that being a permanent freelancer is the dream. Financial independence and career control are. Sometimes gig work gets you there. It's rarely the destination itself.

Use it, don't let it use you.

Red Flags - How to Spot a Toxic Workplace

The Problem

You're sitting in an interview, nodding enthusiastically as the hiring manager describes their "dynamic, fast-paced environment" and "work-hard, play-hard culture." You're so focused on landing the job that you miss the fact that they just told you they expect you to work insane hours and drink away your stress. By the time you realize what you've walked into, you're already trapped in a toxic situation that could have been avoided if you'd known what to look for.

Most people are terrible at recognizing red flags during the hiring process because they're desperate for a job and trained to see any employer interest as validation. You've been conditioned to sell yourself so hard that you forget you're also supposed to be evaluating them. The result is that you end up in workplace situations that slowly destroy your mental health, professional reputation, and financial stability.

The biggest tragedy is that toxic workplaces advertise their toxicity openly. They just use coded language that sounds positive if you don't know how to translate it. Once you understand their secret language, avoiding disaster becomes much easier.

Discussion

Let's start with the classics. When a company says "we're like family here," what they mean is "we'll guilt you into working for free and manipulate you with emotional appeals when you try to set boundaries." Real families don't fire you for missing your quarterly targets. Real families don't make you reapply for your position every year during "restructuring." They're using family language to get you to accept treatment that would be illegal if they were honest about the employment relationship.

"We work hard and play hard" translates to "we have a drinking problem and expect you to develop one too." This is code for a culture where overwork is celebrated, burnout is inevitable, and alcohol is used as both a reward system and a coping mechanism. The "play hard" part usually means mandatory happy hours, team-building events that eat into your personal time, and social pressure to participate in activities that have nothing to do with your job performance.

"Unlimited PTO" is perhaps the most insidious lie in modern corporate America. What it really means is "we've made taking vacation so complicated and guilt-inducing that no one will use it, plus we don't have to pay out accrued vacation when you leave." Companies with unlimited PTO policies see lower vacation usage than companies with traditional policies because employees never feel like they've "earned" the time off and managers make them feel guilty for taking it.

When job postings seek "rockstars," "ninjas," or "gurus," they're telling you they want someone desperate enough to accept terrible working conditions in exchange for a cool title. These aren't descriptions of the job, they're descriptions of their fantasy employee: someone with superhuman abilities who works for regular human compensation. Real professionals don't describe themselves with terms borrowed from entertainment and martial arts.

"Fast-paced environment" is corporate speak for "we have no idea how to plan or manage workload, so everything is a crisis." This usually means poor leadership, unrealistic deadlines, constant firefighting, and a workplace where being busy is more important than being effective. Fast-paced can be energizing when it's the result of genuine growth and opportunity. It's soul-crushing when it's the result of incompetent management.

"Competitive salary" means "below market rate, but we're hoping you don't know that." If the salary were competitive, they'd tell you what it is. When companies are vague about compensation, it's because they know their offer is inadequate and they're hoping to get you emotionally invested before revealing the disappointing reality.

"Flexible hours" often translates to "you'll work nights and weekends but we'll pretend it's a benefit." True flexibility means you have control over when you work. Fake flexibility means they have control over when you work, and when you work happens to be all the time.

"Opportunity to wear many hats" is code for "do three jobs for one salary and be grateful for the experience." This is how companies justify understaffing and role confusion. Wearing many hats can be valuable early in your career when you're learning. It's exploitation when you're an experienced professional being asked to do work that should be handled by multiple people or different departments.

"Young, dynamic team" usually means "age discrimination and inexperience." They're telling you they don't hire older workers and they don't value experience. This often correlates with below-market compensation, unrealistic expectations, and management that doesn't understand how to build sustainable business practices.

"Results-oriented culture" means "we don't care how we destroy you mentally as long as you hit your numbers." This is often code for a workplace where the process doesn't matter, work-life balance is considered weakness, and burnout is seen as a personal failing instead of a management problem.

"Open office concept" translates to "no privacy, constant interruption, and we've read exactly one Harvard Business Review article about collaboration." Open offices are cheaper than providing office space, and companies have convinced themselves that forced interaction leads to innovation. In reality, they lead to decreased productivity, higher stress levels, and more sick days.

"Startup mentality" usually means "expect Fortune 500 results with garage-level resources." This is how established companies try to get employees to accept startup-level compensation and job security while demanding corporate-level performance and availability.

Pay attention to how they talk about previous employees. If they consistently describe people who left as "not a good fit" or say "people leave to pursue other opportunities," they're deflecting responsibility for their turnover problem. Healthy companies talk about former employees with respect and acknowledge that people leave for various legitimate reasons.

During the interview process, watch for hostility from the people you meet, unprepared interviewers who clearly haven't read your resume, and pressure tactics designed to get you to make a quick decision. If they can't be professional during the courtship phase when they're trying to impress you, imagine how they'll treat you once you're hired.

Solutions

The key to avoiding toxic workplaces is to evaluate them as hard as they're evaluating you. You're not just trying to get hired, you're trying to figure out if this is a place where you can succeed and maintain your sanity.

Research the company thoroughly before you interview. Look at their Glassdoor reviews, but understand that companies game these systems by encouraging positive reviews from current employees and disputing negative ones. Look for patterns in the complaints. One person saying the workload is unreasonable might be an outlier. Ten people saying it suggests a systemic problem.

Check their social media presence and recent news coverage. How do they treat negative publicity? How do they respond to criticism? Do they take responsibility for problems or blame external factors? Companies that can't handle criticism from strangers probably can't handle feedback from employees.

During interviews, ask questions that reveal their true culture. "What does work-life balance look like here?" "How do you handle competing priorities and unrealistic deadlines?" "Can you tell me about someone who's succeeded here and what made them successful?" "What happened to the last person in this role?"

Pay attention to the answers, but also pay attention to how long it takes them to answer, their body language, and whether they try to deflect or change the subject. Good companies love talking about their culture because they're proud of it. Toxic companies get defensive when you ask direct questions.

Meet the people you'd be working with directly, not just HR and the hiring manager. How do they seem? Are they enthusiastic about their work? Do they seem stressed or burned out? Are they able to speak freely about their experience, or do they give canned answers that sound like they're being monitored?

Look at their employee retention and promotion practices. How long do people stay? Are there people who've been promoted from within, or do they only hire externally for senior positions? If everyone seems to have been there less than two years, that's a red flag.

Get everything in writing before you accept an offer. Job responsibilities, compensation, benefits, vacation policy, performance expectations. If they're reluctant to put something in writing, it's probably because they plan to change it later.

Trust your instincts. If something feels off during the interview process, it's probably because something is off. Don't ignore red flags because you need a job. A toxic workplace can damage your career, your health, and your financial situation far more than being unemployed for a few extra weeks while you find something better.

Exercises

Create a red flag checklist based on your past experiences and the warning signs we've discussed. Use this checklist during every interview process to help you stay objective when you're emotionally invested in getting the job.

Practice asking tough questions in low-stakes situations so you're comfortable asking them when it matters. Role-play interviews with friends or family members who can help you refine your approach.

Research five companies in your field that you'd never want to work for. Study their job postings, websites, and employee reviews to identify the language patterns and warning signs you want to avoid.

Develop a standard research process you can use for every potential employer. What sources will you check? What questions will you ask? What information do you need to make an informed decision?

Create a non-negotiable requirements list for your next job. Not wish-list items, but absolute requirements. Use this list to evaluate opportunities and avoid compromising on things that matter to your long-term success and happiness.

The best time to evaluate a workplace is before you're financially dependent on it. Once you're hired, leaving becomes costly and complicated, and you start rationalizing things you never would have accepted in the interview. Do your homework upfront.

A few extra weeks of job searching is always better than months or years in a toxic workplace that slowly destroys everything you've worked to build.

Surviving the Disposable Workforce Mentality

"Job security is gone. The driving force of a career must come from the individual." - Homa Bahrami

The Problem

Companies now view employees as expendable resources to be optimized for quarterly results, regardless of performance or loyalty. You could be employee of the month, exceed all your targets, and work weekends without complaint, and still get laid off if some analyst in a spreadsheet decides your department is 3% over budget. The old social contract where hard work and loyalty guaranteed job security is dead, but nobody sent you the memo.

The most insidious part is how they've reframed mass layoffs as business optimization instead of human devastation. They call it "rightsizing," "restructuring," "strategic realignment," or "digital transformation." They announce layoffs in the same breath as record profits, executive bonuses, and stock buybacks. They've made disposing of human beings sound like responsible financial management.

Meanwhile, they expect you to maintain the same level of passion, commitment, and loyalty as if the old contract still existed. They want you to work like you own the company while treating you like a line item they can delete at any moment. The psychological whiplash of being told you're "family" while being treated as disposable is enough to drive anyone insane.

Discussion

Let's talk about what "rightsizing" really means. It means they hired too many people when times were good and now they're correcting their mistake by destroying lives instead of taking responsibility for poor planning. It means they promised investors growth rates that can only be achieved by cutting labor costs. It means executives get bonuses for hitting profit targets that were only possible by firing the people who created the value in the first place.

The AI excuse has become popular lately. "It's not personal, it's technological progress." They act like AI appeared overnight and forced their hand, when in reality they've been planning these cuts for months or years. AI gives them cover to do what they wanted to do anyway: reduce labor costs and increase profits. The technology isn't replacing jobs because it's better, it's replacing jobs because it's cheaper.

Performance doesn't protect you when algorithms don't have feelings. You can be the best employee in your department and still get cut because you're in the wrong cost center or your salary is above the median for your role. The spreadsheet doesn't care that you've never missed a deadline or that you trained half the team. It only cares about numbers, and if your number is too high, you're gone.

The layoff announcement is always the same performance. The CEO gets on a video call looking appropriately somber and talks about difficult decisions and market conditions. They thank everyone for their dedication and hard work while explaining why that dedication and hard work isn't enough to keep you employed. They talk about supporting affected employees through the transition, which usually means two weeks of severance and access to a job placement service that sends generic LinkedIn messages.

The survivors get a separate message about how this positions the company for future growth and how everyone remaining is now part of a leaner, more efficient organization. Translation: congratulations, you get to do your job plus the job of the person sitting next to you who got laid off. Don't worry, you won't get their salary too, but you will get the privilege of working twice as hard for the same pay.

The timing is always strategic. Companies love Friday layoffs because it gives people the weekend to process the shock before they can network or file unemployment claims. They love end-of-quarter layoffs because it makes the numbers look good for earnings calls. They love holiday season layoffs because people are too distracted to organize or push back effectively.

The security theater is galling. They'll have security escort people out like they're criminals who might steal office supplies or sabotage the coffee machine. People who've worked there for years get treated like potential threats the moment they're no longer useful. Your badge gets deactivated, your email gets shut off, and you're suddenly persona non grata in a place where you spent most of your waking hours.

The "it's just business" mentality ignores the human cost of these decisions. People lose their homes, their healthcare, their sense of identity and purpose. Families get destroyed. Communities get devastated when major employers pull out. But none of that shows up in the quarterly earnings report, so it doesn't matter to the decision makers.

The most infuriating part is how they frame it as an opportunity. "This is a chance for you to explore new opportunities and find something even better." Right, getting fired is doing you a favor. You should be grateful that they're freeing you up to pursue your dreams. It's like someone burning down your house and telling you it's an opportunity to upgrade your living situation.

Solutions

Since loyalty is dead and job security is an illusion, your only protection is preparation. You need to see layoffs coming before they happen, position yourself to survive if possible, and maximize your exit package if survival isn't an option.

Learn to read the early warning signs. Companies telegraph layoffs months before they happen if you know what to look for. Hiring freezes, budget cuts, consultant visits, leadership changes, and vague announcements about "strategic reviews" are all red flags. When executives start talking about efficiency and optimization, start updating your resume.

Pay attention to the financial indicators. Declining revenue, missed targets, increased debt, or pressure from investors all increase layoff risk. Companies rarely lay people off when business is booming, but they love to use economic uncertainty as cover for cuts they wanted to make anyway.

Watch for organizational changes that signal trouble. New leadership often means new priorities and new cost structures. Mergers and acquisitions almost always mean redundancies. Consulting firms that specialize in "organizational efficiency" are basically layoff planning services.

Listen to what executives say in earnings calls and investor meetings. They often announce layoff intentions months before they announce them to employees. They'll talk about "optimizing headcount" or "achieving operational efficiency" or "streamlining operations." This is your advance warning.

Document everything obsessively. Keep records of your contributions, achievements, and positive feedback. Save emails that show your value to the organization. Track projects you've completed and problems you've solved. If you get laid off, this documentation becomes evidence for severance negotiations and unemployment claims.

Build relationships with decision makers who can protect you or give you advance warning. The people who survive layoffs usually have advocates in senior management or critical skills that are hard to replace. You can't control everything, but you can position yourself as someone who's expensive to lose.

Develop skills that transfer across industries and companies. The more versatile you are, the faster you can find new opportunities. Focus on capabilities that complement AI instead of competing with it. Become the person who manages the technology, not the person replaced by it.

Maintain an active professional network even when you're employed. The best time to network is when you don't need anything. Invest in relationships with people who could hire you or recommend you. Keep your LinkedIn profile updated. Stay visible in your industry through conferences, publications, or professional associations.

Keep your finances in survival mode. The old rule was six months of expenses in emergency savings. The new rule is twelve months because job searches take longer and severance packages are smaller. Live below your means and avoid debt that could force you to take the first job offer you get.

Negotiate your severance package aggressively. Everything is negotiable, especially if you have documentation of your value or evidence of company wrongdoing. Don't sign anything immediately. Consult with an employment lawyer if the package seems inadequate. Companies often offer more than their initial package if you push back professionally.

Plan your own exit timeline. Instead of waiting to get laid off, start looking for better opportunities while you're still employed. You have more leverage when you're negotiating from a position of strength. Getting laid off is almost never a surprise if you're paying attention to the warning signs.

Exercises

Create a layoff early warning system for your workplace. What metrics should you track? What organizational changes should you monitor? What sources of information can give you advance notice? Develop a systematic way to stay informed about your company's financial health and strategic direction.

Audit your current job security honestly. How replaceable are you? How critical are your skills? How strong are your relationships with decision makers? How vulnerable is your department to cuts? Use this assessment to identify areas where you need to build more security.

Develop a rapid job search capability. Update your resume quarterly whether you need it or not. Maintain a portfolio of work samples and achievement documentation. Keep your professional references current. Practice interviewing skills regularly so you're ready when opportunities arise.

Build a personal board of directors: people in your network who can provide career advice, job referrals, and industry intelligence. Maintain these relationships consistently, not just when you need something. Be generous with your own help and introductions so people are willing to help you when you need it.

Calculate your financial runway and create a plan to extend it. How long could you survive without income? What expenses could you cut immediately? What assets could you liquidate if necessary? Having a clear financial survival plan reduces the panic and desperation that lead to bad career decisions.

The disposable workforce mentality isn't your fault, but surviving it is your responsibility. Companies will continue to treat employees as expendable resources as long as it's profitable to do so. Your job is to make yourself as unexpendable as possible while preparing for the possibility that even unexpendable isn't enough.

The goal isn't to find a secure job. Secure jobs don't exist anymore. The goal is to build personal security that doesn't depend on any single employer's goodwill or business model.

You are not disposable, even if they treat you like you are. Act accordingly.

Gaming the Work-Life Balance Illusion

"The challenge of work-life balance is without question one of the most significant struggles faced by modern man." - *Stephen Covey*

The Problem

Work-life balance has become the biggest scam in corporate America. Companies love talking about it because it makes them sound enlightened and employee-friendly, but what they really mean is "work more efficiently so we can give you more work." They've turned the concept into a productivity hack where the goal isn't to work less, but to work better so you can work more without completely losing your mind.

The dirty secret is that work-life balance, as sold by corporations, doesn't exist. What exists is work-life integration, where work gradually consumes every aspect of your life until you can't tell where work ends and life begins. Your phone is always on. Your laptop comes home every night. Your vacation includes "just checking email" every few hours. You're always available, always thinking about work, always slightly anxious about what might be happening while you're not working.

The worst part is that they've convinced you this is your fault. If you're stressed, it's because you haven't mastered time management. If you're working late, it's because you're not efficient enough. If you can't disconnect on weekends, it's because you lack boundaries. They've made work-life balance a personal failing instead of a systemic problem.

Discussion

Let's talk about what work-life balance propaganda really means. When companies say they support work-life balance, they mean they want you to be so efficient during work hours that you can handle an impossible workload without completely burning out. They don't want you to work less. They want you to work smarter so you can work the same amount without quitting or having a nervous breakdown.

The "flexible schedule" benefit is a perfect example. They'll let you work from 7 AM to 4 PM instead of 9 AM to 6 PM, but you're still working nine hours a day. They'll let you work from home on Fridays, but you're expected to be available for calls and emails all day. They'll let you take your laptop to your kid's soccer game, but you'd better be monitoring Slack in case something "urgent" comes up.

The always-on culture has become so normalized that being unreachable is considered unprofessional. You're expected to respond to emails within an hour, even on weekends. You're expected to join calls from vacation because "it's just thirty minutes." You're expected to check messages after hours because "I know you're not working, but..." The technology that was supposed to give us flexibility has become a digital leash that keeps us connected to work 24/7.

Remote work has made this even worse. Companies discovered that people working from home often work longer hours than people in the office because there's no clear separation between work space and personal space. Your dining table becomes your conference room. Your bedroom becomes your office. Your living room becomes your break room. You never really leave work because work lives in your house now.

I learned this lesson directly. Early in my career I went to my boss Fred and made two reasonable points: I deserved some form of additional compensation for being on call 24 hours a day, 7 days a week, 365 days a year, and I was going to hike Joshua Tree for a weekend and would be out of cell range. Not asking permission. It was my time. Fred didn't consider either point. He yelled. He told me that if I didn't respond to a page and call back within 15 minutes I would be fired. Compensation was off the table. Joshua Tree was off the table. The

conversation was over. That was work-life balance in practice —
not a policy, not a program, just a direct statement of who
owned my time and what it would cost me to forget it.

The "unlimited PTO" scam is another perfect example of how
companies manipulate the work-life balance conversation. They
give you unlimited vacation days but create a culture where
taking vacation is seen as letting the team down. They don't
track your days off, which means they also don't encourage you
to take them. Most people with unlimited PTO take fewer
vacation days than people with traditional policies because they
never feel like they've "earned" the time off.

Then there's the wellness program theater. Companies offer
yoga classes and meditation apps while expecting you to work
sixty-hour weeks. They provide healthy snacks in the break
room while scheduling back-to-back meetings through lunch.
They talk about mental health awareness while creating work
environments that destroy mental health. It's like offering
band-aids while continuing to stab you.

The real con is how they've made work-life balance your
responsibility to figure out. They'll give you time management
training instead of reducing your workload. They'll offer stress
management seminars instead of addressing the sources of
stress. They'll provide employee assistance programs instead of
creating sustainable work environments. The message is clear:
if you can't handle the workload, it's your problem, not theirs.

Burnout has been rebranded as a personal weakness instead of
a predictable result of unsustainable work practices. If you're
exhausted, you need better self-care. If you're overwhelmed,
you need better priorities. If you're working weekends, you need
better time management. The system isn't broken, you're just
not optimized enough to handle it.

The pizza party cure is the ultimate insult. When morale is low
and people are burning out, companies throw a pizza party or
organize a team-building event instead of addressing the
workload, compensation, or management issues causing the
problems. It's like putting a fresh coat of paint on a house with

a cracked foundation and acting like you've solved the structural problem.

Solutions

Real work-life balance isn't something your employer gives you. It's something you create and defend. Set boundaries that work for you and enforce them consistently, regardless of what the company culture expects.

Start small and be strategic about it. Pick one boundary you can realistically maintain and defend it consistently. Maybe you don't check email after 8 PM. Maybe you don't work on Sundays. Maybe you don't respond to non-urgent messages on vacation. Choose something that matters to you and stick to it without apology or explanation.

Train people on your availability by being consistently unavailable during your personal time. Don't respond to non-urgent emails immediately just because you saw them. Don't answer work calls during dinner just because your phone rang. Don't check Slack while you're watching a movie just because you heard a notification. People will adapt to your boundaries if you maintain them consistently.

Learn to appear always available while protecting your time. Set up auto-responders that make it look like you're on top of your email without checking it constantly. Schedule emails to send during business hours even if you write them at weird times. Use status messages and calendar blocking to manage expectations about when you're reachable.

Create physical and mental separation between work and personal time, especially if you work from home. Have a dedicated workspace that you can close off at the end of the day. Develop a shutdown ritual that helps you transition from work mode to personal mode. Change clothes, take a walk, or do something that signals to your brain that work is over.

When you take vacation, really take vacation. Set up proper coverage for your responsibilities. Turn on an out-of-office message that sets realistic expectations for when you'll respond. Don't check email "just for a few minutes" because those few minutes turn into hours and you're never really disconnected.

Negotiate your workload, not just your schedule. Flexible hours don't help if you have sixty hours of work to do every week. If your employer wants you to be more efficient, make them define what that means in terms of outcomes and priorities. If everything is urgent, then nothing is urgent. Make them choose what matters most.

Document the cost of their unrealistic expectations. Track how much time you're spending on different tasks. Note when deadline conflicts force you to work overtime. Keep records of how workload affects quality and timelines. When you can show the concrete impact of poor planning and unrealistic expectations, you have leverage to negotiate better conditions.

Use their wellness resources strategically, but don't let them substitute for systemic changes. Take advantage of mental health benefits, flexible spending accounts, and employee assistance programs. But don't let them pretend that offering these benefits solves the problem of unsustainable work practices.

The goal isn't to find perfect balance. Perfect balance doesn't exist. The goal is to create conditions where work serves your life instead of consuming it. Some weeks you'll work more, some weeks you'll work less. Some projects will require extra effort, some periods will be more relaxed. The key is making sure that the intense periods are the exception, not the rule.

Exercises

Audit your current work-life integration honestly. How many hours are you really working each week? How often do you check email outside of work hours? How much of your personal time is interrupted by work thoughts or tasks? How much vacation do you take, and how disconnected are you when you take it?

Identify your personal non-negotiables. What aspects of your personal life are you not willing to sacrifice for work? Family dinners? Weekend mornings? Vacation time? Exercise? Once you know what matters most to you, you can be strategic about protecting it.

Track your productivity patterns to understand when you do your best work. Are you more effective in the morning or afternoon? Do you get more done in shorter, focused sessions or longer blocks of time? Use this information to optimize your schedule and push back on meeting requests that conflict with your peak productivity times.

Practice saying no to non-essential requests. Start with small things and work your way up to bigger boundaries. "I can't make that 7 PM call, but I'm available tomorrow morning." "I won't be checking email this weekend, but I'll prioritize your request first thing Monday." "I can take on that project, but something else will need to come off my plate."

Create accountability systems that help you stick to your boundaries. Tell people about your work-life balance goals. Ask friends or family to call you out when you're checking email during personal time. Set up automatic reminders to leave work at a reasonable hour.

Boundaries aren't selfish. They're necessary for sustainable performance. You can't do good work if you're exhausted, stressed, and resentful.

The companies that respect boundaries and support real work-life balance are the ones worth working for. The companies that push back against reasonable boundaries are telling you everything you need to know about their values and priorities.

Your time and energy are finite resources. Use them strategically.

Navigating the Hierarchy of Exploitation

---

*"Power corrupts, and absolute power corrupts absolutely." -
Lord Acton*

The Problem

Every company has a hierarchy designed to extract maximum value from employees while minimizing their ability to push back. Middle management exists to be the enforcement arm of executive decisions, HR exists to protect the company from legal liability, and the whole system is designed to make you feel like any problems you're having are your fault, not theirs.

Understanding this hierarchy isn't about becoming cynical or paranoid. It's about recognizing the game so you can play it strategically instead of being played by it. Most people stumble through their careers wondering why hard work doesn't pay off, why politics matter more than performance, and why "culture fit" seems to exclude anyone who asks uncomfortable questions.

The hierarchy of exploitation works because each level has different incentives that rarely align with your interests. What's good for the C-suite isn't good for middle management. What's good for middle management definitely isn't good for you. What's good for HR is almost never good for anyone except HR. Once you understand these misaligned incentives, you can stop taking workplace dysfunction personally and start navigating it strategically.

Discussion

Let's start with middle management, the people who have just enough power to make your life miserable but not enough power to fix anything. They're caught between unrealistic demands from above and limited resources below. Their job is to somehow make the impossible happen while absorbing all the stress and blame when things go wrong.

Middle managers didn't choose to be the enforcement arm of corporate policy. They're just trying to survive in a system that holds them accountable for results they can't control with resources they don't have. When they tell you that your project timeline is non-negotiable, it's because someone above them said the same thing. When they can't approve your raise request, it's because someone above them controls the budget. When they seem to micromanage everything, it's because someone above them is micromanaging them.

The shit flows downhill principle is real and relentless. Executives make promises to investors. Investors pressure executives. Executives pressure VPs. VPs pressure directors. Directors pressure managers. Managers pressure you. Everyone in the chain is just trying to avoid being the person who disappoints the person above them, which means the person at the bottom of the chain (you) gets all the pressure and none of the power.

Middle managers develop survival strategies that often make them seem incompetent or malicious when they're just responding to incentives. They become experts at managing up instead of managing their teams because their performance reviews depend on keeping their boss happy, not keeping you happy. They learn to over-promise and under-deliver because saying no to unrealistic requests is career suicide. They master the art of taking credit for successes while deflecting blame for failures because that's how they stay employed.

Your manager's primary job isn't to support your career development or ensure your happiness. Their primary job is to extract productivity from you while protecting themselves from any negative consequences of that extraction. They want you to be good enough to make them look competent but not so good that you threaten their position or make them look replaceable.

I've had a handful of genuinely good managers over my career. The only one who stands out without reservation is Steve Davis.

Everyone else flowed it down. Every time something went wrong, it was their people's fault. That pattern is almost universal once you know to look for it.

But sometimes the constraint isn't cowardice, it's semantics — and the difference matters. A manager named Al hired me to get a project back on track. The problem was one engineer who was using it as a personal playground to test his programming ideas. The project was over a million dollars over budget and five years late. I told Al he needed to fire the guy. Al kept saying he couldn't. I heard this for months before I listened to the actual word: couldn't. Not won't. Couldn't. I requested a promotion that would put me in the problem engineer's management chain. Al approved it. My first act in the new role was to fire him. Sometimes the manager above you isn't refusing to act — they just need someone else to be the one who acts.

HR operates on a completely different set of incentives that are almost always opposed to yours. Despite all the employee engagement surveys and workplace culture initiatives, HR's real job is to minimize the company's legal and financial liability. They're not your advocate, they're the company's defense attorney.

When HR talks about being a "business partner," they mean they see themselves as part of the business, not part of the workforce. They're management, not labor. Their success is measured by how well they protect the company from employee-related problems, not by how well they solve employee problems. Keeping you happy only matters when unhappy employees create legal or retention risks.

The open-door policy is a perfect example of how HR creates the illusion of advocacy while serving their real function. They want you to come to them with problems so they can assess whether those problems pose a threat to the company. They're not gathering information to help you, they're gathering information to protect the company from you.

HR loves policies and procedures because they create defensible decision-making processes. When you complain about unfair treatment, they can point to the policy manual and explain how everything was done correctly according to established procedures. They're not interested in whether the policies are fair or effective, only in whether following them protects the company from lawsuits.

The "culture fit" concept is insidious because it gives companies a legal way to discriminate against anyone who doesn't conform to their preferred employee profile. Culture fit usually means willing to accept low pay, long hours, and poor treatment without complaining. It means someone who won't ask uncomfortable questions about pay equity, working conditions, or management competence.

Office politics aren't a bug in the system, they're a feature. The informal power structure often matters more than the official org chart because that's where real decisions get made. The person with the CEO's ear has more influence than the person with the director title. The person who gets invited to the golf outings has more access than the person who just does excellent work.

Networking isn't about making friends, it's about building alliances that can protect you when the inevitable reorganization happens. The people who survive layoffs aren't the best performers, they're the people who are connected to decision makers. Merit matters, but relationships matter more.

The meritocracy myth keeps people believing that hard work and good performance will be rewarded, when in reality advancement often depends on factors that have nothing to do with competence. Nepotism is alive and well in corporate America, it's just disguised as cultural fit and leadership potential.

Solutions

The key to navigating this hierarchy is to understand what each level really wants and give them just enough of it to protect yourself while building what you need to advance your own agenda.

For middle management, make your boss look good while building evidence of your own competence. Help them solve their problems, meet their deadlines, and avoid surprises that could embarrass them in front of their boss. But document your contributions so you get credit for your work and build a reputation that extends beyond your immediate manager.

Learn to manage up without losing your dignity. This doesn't mean becoming a sycophant or sacrificing your integrity. It means understanding your manager's pressures and priorities so you can position your requests in terms they care about. If they're worried about hitting quarterly targets, frame your proposals in terms of quarterly impact. If they're concerned about team morale, emphasize how your idea will improve team satisfaction.

Build relationships across the organization, not just with your direct manager. Having allies in different departments gives you options when your immediate situation becomes untenable. It also gives you access to information about opportunities that might not be visible from your current position.

For HR, become the employee who never creates problems for them. Follow policies precisely, document everything, and handle conflicts professionally. But remember that everything you say to HR can and will be used to protect the company, not you. Be friendly but not confiding. Be helpful but not naive.

When you need to escalate issues to HR, come prepared with documentation and proposed solutions. Don't just complain about problems, demonstrate that you've tried to resolve them appropriately and need their help with obstacles. Make it easy for them to help you by showing that helping you serves the company's interests.

Understand the informal power structure and invest in relationships that matter. Who influences decision-making? Who has access to senior leadership? Who knows about opportunities before they're posted? These people aren't the ones with impressive titles, but they're the ones who can open doors or provide early warnings about changes.

Play the culture fit game strategically. You don't have to sacrifice your values or authenticity, but you do need to understand what behaviors and attitudes are rewarded in your workplace. If collaboration is valued, be collaborative. If innovation is rewarded, be innovative. If loyalty is expected, demonstrate loyalty. But do all of this while maintaining your own standards and building skills that transfer to other environments.

Build your own informal network of people who share information and look out for each other. These relationships should be based on mutual benefit, not one-sided dependence. Share opportunities, provide references, and offer support to others so they're willing to do the same for you.

Exercises

Map the real power structure in your organization. Who makes decisions about budgets, hiring, and strategic direction? Who influences those decisions? Who has access to senior leadership? Understanding the informal hierarchy helps you focus your relationship-building efforts where they'll have the most impact.

Assess your current relationship with your manager honestly. Are you making their life easier or harder? Do they see you as part of the solution or part of the problem? How can you better support their goals while advancing your own?

Audit your HR interactions to make sure you're protecting yourself appropriately. Are you documenting important conversations? Are you following policies correctly? Are you creating any legal or compliance risks that could make you a target?

Identify the informal influencers in your workplace and develop strategies for building relationships with them. Understanding who actually runs things isn't paranoia, it's situational awareness.

Create a plan for building your reputation beyond your current role. How can people outside your department learn about your capabilities? What opportunities exist for cross-functional work, speaking at company events, or contributing to high-visibility projects?

The hierarchy of exploitation isn't personal, it's structural. People respond to incentives you might not see. Understanding those dynamics means you stop being surprised when they act accordingly.

You're not trying to become a master manipulator or office politician. You're trying to understand the game well enough to protect yourself while building the skills, relationships, and reputation you need to create better options.

Work the system, don't let the system work you.

Dealing with Sociopathic Leadership

"The best way to find out if you can trust somebody is to trust them." - Ernest Hemingway (Note: This doesn't apply at work)

The Problem

There's a disturbing correlation between excecutive success and personality disorders. The traits that make someone a clinical sociopath (charm, manipulation, lack of empathy, grandiosity) are often the same traits that help them climb corporate ladders. They're promoted for being "decisive" when they're ruthless. They're praised for being "visionary" when they're delusional. They're celebrated for being "results-oriented" when they're willing to destroy anyone who gets in their way.

Working for a sociopathic boss isn't just unpleasant, it's dangerous. They don't see you as a human being with needs, feelings, and limitations. You're a tool to be used until you break, then discarded and replaced. They'll take credit for your successes, blame you for their failures, and gaslight you into believing that your perfectly reasonable reactions to their unreasonable behavior are signs of your inadequacy.

The most insidious part is how they've learned to weaponize corporate culture to enable their dysfunction. They hide behind "high standards" and "performance culture" while creating work environments that would be considered abusive in any other context. They've figured out how to be monsters while maintaining plausible deniability.

Discussion

Let's start by understanding what you're dealing with. A sociopathic boss isn't just someone who's demanding or difficult. They're someone who genuinely lacks empathy and sees other people as objects to be manipulated for their benefit. They're charming when it serves their purposes and cruel when it doesn't. They feel no guilt about lying, cheating, or destroying someone's career if it advances their agenda.

They're masters of impression management. They know exactly how to present themselves to senior leadership, clients, and other stakeholders. They're articulate, confident, and persuasive. They tell people what they want to hear and make promises they have no intention of keeping. They're often genuinely talented at certain aspects of their job, which makes their dysfunction harder to identify and address.

The charm offensive is usually how they operate with people who have power over them or people they're trying to recruit. They'll be incredibly attentive, supportive, and encouraging during the interview process or when they need something from you. They'll make you feel special, valued, and chosen. This isn't genuine appreciation, it's a calculated investment in getting what they want from you.

Once they have you trapped (either because you've accepted the job or because leaving would be costly), the mask starts to slip. The charm gets replaced with manipulation, criticism, and psychological warfare. They'll move the goalposts constantly so you can never quite succeed. They'll give you impossible tasks with unrealistic deadlines and then blame you when you can't deliver miracles.

The gaslighting is perhaps their most dangerous weapon. They'll make you question your own memory, judgment, and competence. They'll deny conversations that happened, claim they never made promises they clearly made, and reframe your successes as their successes while making your failures entirely your responsibility. They'll convince you that your perfectly normal reactions to their abnormal behavior are signs that you're not cut out for this level of responsibility.

They love creating artificial urgency and crisis because it keeps people off-balance and prevents them from thinking clearly.

Everything is always urgent, critical, and time-sensitive. There's never time to plan properly, gather adequate resources, or think through the implications of decisions. This chaos serves their purposes because it makes people dependent on their "decisive leadership" and prevents anyone from questioning their methods.

The divide-and-conquer strategy is another favorite. They'll pit team members against each other, share confidential information selectively to create drama, and use favoritism to ensure that no one feels secure enough to challenge them. They want people competing for their approval instead of collaborating effectively, because collaboration might expose their incompetence.

They're experts at taking credit and deflecting blame. Your successes become evidence of their excellent leadership and strategic vision. Your failures become evidence of your inadequacy and lack of commitment. They'll throw you under the bus without hesitation if it protects their reputation or advances their agenda.

The emotional manipulation is constant and sophisticated. They'll use guilt, fear, anger, and false intimacy to control your behavior. They'll make you feel like you're letting them down personally when you can't meet impossible demands. They'll share personal information or create a false sense of friendship to make you feel obligated to accept treatment you would never tolerate from a stranger.

They thrive on having information and using it strategically. They'll pump you for details about your personal life, financial situation, career goals, and relationships with other employees. This isn't because they care about you as a person, it's because information is leverage. They want to know what buttons to push and what vulnerabilities to exploit.

The performance review becomes a weapon in their hands. They'll use it to rewrite history, create false narratives about your performance, and set you up for failure. They'll document problems that don't exist, ignore achievements that do exist, and create improvement plans designed to be impossible to fulfill.

Solutions

Protecting yourself from a sociopathic boss requires a fundamentally different strategy than dealing with a merely difficult manager. You can't fix them, reason with them, or appeal to their better nature. You can only protect yourself while building an exit strategy.

Document everything obsessively. Keep records of all conversations, emails, promises, and commitments. Take notes during meetings and send follow-up emails confirming what was discussed. Save text messages and voicemails. Create a paper trail that can protect you if they try to rewrite history or blame you for their failures.

Never give them ammunition they can use against you. Don't share personal information, don't confide in them about your concerns or frustrations, and don't give them insight into your vulnerabilities. Be professional but not personal. They will use anything you tell them as a weapon when it serves their purposes.

Build relationships with other people in the organization who can serve as witnesses and advocates. You need allies who can verify your version of events and vouch for your competence. Sociopathic bosses often isolate their targets, so maintaining external relationships is crucial for your survival.

Set boundaries and enforce them consistently, even when they push back. They will test your limits constantly to see how much abuse you'll accept. Don't make threats you can't follow through on, but be clear about what you will and won't do. They respect strength and exploit weakness.

Focus on protecting your reputation and building evidence of your competence. Make sure other people see your work and understand your contributions. Volunteer for cross-functional projects, present at company meetings, and create visibility beyond your immediate team. You want people to know who you are and what you're capable of independent of your boss's narrative.

Don't try to expose them or get them fired unless you have overwhelming evidence and strong institutional support. Sociopaths are usually skilled at managing up and have convinced senior leadership that they're valuable. Your accusations will likely backfire and make you a target for retaliation.

Plan your exit strategy from day one. Update your resume regularly, maintain your professional network, build your savings, and keep your skills current. The goal isn't to survive indefinitely under a sociopathic boss, it's to survive long enough to create better options for yourself.

When you do leave, don't burn bridges publicly. Sociopathic bosses have long memories and extensive networks. They will try to damage your reputation if they perceive you as a threat. Take the high road, give appropriate notice, and transition your responsibilities professionally.

Exercises

Learn to recognize the early warning signs of sociopathic leadership so you can avoid these situations in the future. How do they treat people who can't help them? How do they talk about former employees? Do their stories about their successes seem credible? Are they charming in a way that feels calculated instead of genuine?

Create a comprehensive documentation system for all interactions with your boss. What format will you use? How will you store the information securely? How will you organize it so you can find incidents quickly? Consistency is key to building a credible record.

Build a support network of colleagues who can provide perspective and validation. Working for a sociopath can make you question your own judgment and competence. Having trusted colleagues who can confirm that the behavior you're experiencing is not normal helps maintain your sanity.

Develop stress management techniques that can help you cope with the psychological toll of working for someone who sees you as disposable. This might include therapy, meditation, exercise, or other activities that help you maintain your mental health while dealing with a toxic situation.

Create plans for protecting your work and reputation. How will you ensure that your contributions are visible to other people? How will you document your achievements in ways that can't be erased or minimized? How will you build relationships that can provide references and opportunities when you're ready to leave?

Sociopathic bosses target people they perceive as vulnerable. Become someone who's too costly to attack. Build your skills, document your value, maintain your network, and always have an exit plan. You can't change them, but you can make yourself a harder target.

The goal isn't to win against a sociopath. The goal is to survive with your sanity, reputation, and career prospects intact while you build something better.

Don't try to beat them at their own game. Play a different game entirely.

Your Coworkers Are Not Your Friends

"Keep your friends close, but your coworkers at a professional distance." - Anonymous

---

The Problem

The modern workplace pushes the myth that your colleagues should be your chosen family, your support system, and your social circle all rolled into one. Companies love promoting team bonding, work friendships, and "bringing your whole self to work" because it creates emotional investment that makes you less likely to leave and more willing to accept poor treatment in the name of loyalty to people you care about.

But workplace relationships are fundamentally transactional, no matter how genuine they feel in the moment. Your coworkers' primary obligation is to their own career survival, not to your wellbeing. When layoffs come, when promotions are on the line, or when someone needs a scapegoat, even the nicest people will protect themselves first. Understanding this doesn't make you cynical, it makes you realistic.

The "work family" concept is manipulation designed to extract free emotional labor from you. Real families don't fire you for missing your targets. Real families don't make you reapply for your position during restructuring. Real families don't ask you to relocate across the country or accept a pay cut "for the good of the family." Companies use family language to get family-level loyalty while offering employee-level commitment in return.

Discussion

I've had this confirmed so many times it stopped surprising me. Every time I left a job, and every time colleagues left while I stayed, the friendship ended with the employment. Not one person maintained contact. Not one. The shared context disappeared and so did the relationship. That's not a failure on anyone's part — it's just the honest nature of what those relationships were.

The harder lesson came from Kevin. I put him in charge of desktop support. He was good at it and I considered him a friend. Then I started noticing that he was spending a disproportionate amount of time on the CEO's equipment while his other responsibilities slipped. Users complained. Managers flagged it. I told Kevin directly: if this pattern continued, he'd be fired. His response was to tell me I should probably check with his buddy the CEO before I did anything. I hadn't known Kevin was cultivating that relationship. He'd done it quietly, over time, as an insurance policy. That was the moment I understood that what I'd taken for friendship had been, at least in part, a hedge. When Kevin was eventually fired anyway, the CEO shrugged. Didn't intervene, didn't push back, didn't care. The relationship Kevin had spent years building provided zero protection when it actually mattered.

That's not an unusual story. It's just an unusually clear version of how these relationships work.

Let's talk about what work friendships really are. They're relationships of convenience and proximity, formed between people who might have nothing in common except showing up to the same building every day. You bond over shared frustrations with management, common deadlines, and the mutual experience of workplace absurdity. These relationships can be enjoyable and even meaningful, but they're built on a foundation of mutual professional interest, not genuine personal compatibility.

The problem starts when you forget that these relationships exist within a competitive framework. You're all competing for the same promotions, raises, and opportunities. You're all trying to look good to the same managers. You're all vulnerable to the same layoffs and restructuring. No matter how much you genuinely like each other, these underlying realities create conflicts of interest that don't exist in real friendships.

Information is currency in the workplace, and sharing too much of it with coworkers is like giving away money. When you complain about your boss to a colleague, you're creating information they could use against you if it serves their interests. When you share your salary, your job search activities, or your career frustrations, you're giving them insight into your vulnerabilities and strategies that they might need to exploit later.

The "work wife" or "work husband" phenomenon is dangerous because it creates the illusion of unconditional support in a fundamentally conditional environment. You start trusting someone with confidential information, personal struggles, and career concerns because the relationship feels special and intimate. But when push comes to shove, work relationships are governed by professional necessities, not personal loyalties.

Office gossip feels like harmless social bonding, but it's a weapon that will eventually be turned on you. Today you're bonding with Veronica over stories about how incompetent your manager is. Tomorrow Veronica might be interviewing for your manager's job and using those conversations to demonstrate her loyalty by reporting your "negativity" to senior leadership. The same information that felt like friendship feels like betrayal when the incentives change.

The lunch group, the happy hour crew, and the office chat thread create in-groups and out-groups that affect your professional standing whether you realize it or not. If you're not part of the social circle, you miss informal information about opportunities, changes, and office politics. If you are part of it, you become associated with the group's reputation and get dragged into their conflicts and dramas.

Team building exercises and company social events are designed to blur the boundaries between personal and professional relationships. They want you to feel connected to your coworkers on a personal level so you'll work harder, accept lower pay, and think twice before leaving for a better opportunity. The more invested you are in workplace relationships, the harder it becomes to make rational career decisions.

The helping culture creates obligations that rarely get reciprocated fairly. You stay late to help a colleague finish their project because you're "friends." You cover for someone when they're struggling because you care about them. You share your expertise and connections because it feels like the right thing to do. But when you need help, they're suddenly too busy, too stressed, or too focused on their own priorities to return the favor.

Performance reviews and promotion decisions reveal the true nature of workplace relationships. Suddenly, the person who was your lunch buddy is competing directly with you for a promotion. The colleague who complained about the company with you is now highlighting their own loyalty and commitment while subtly undermining your reputation. The friend who knew about your job search is now using that information to position themselves as more committed to the team.

The departure test is the ultimate reality check for workplace relationships. When someone leaves the company, how many of their work friendships survive? Most workplace relationships evaporate within months because they were based on shared context and mutual professional benefit, not genuine personal connection. The people who really matter will stay in touch. The work friends will gradually stop responding to texts and fade from your life.

Solutions

The goal isn't to be antisocial or paranoid. The goal is to maintain appropriate professional boundaries that protect your interests while still building the relationships you need to succeed. You can be friendly without being friends, collaborative without being vulnerable, and helpful without being exploited.

Be pleasant, professional, and reasonably social without sharing information that could be used against you. Participate in office conversations about neutral topics: weekend plans, TV shows, sports, current events. Avoid discussions about salaries, job searches, boss complaints, company criticism, or personal problems that could affect your professional reputation.

Create information boundaries that protect your strategic interests. Don't discuss your career plans, financial situation, job search activities, or concerns about the company with coworkers. These conversations might feel like friendship, but they're creating intelligence that could be used to undermine you later.

Build work relationships based on mutual professional benefit instead of personal intimacy. Help colleagues when it serves your interests, ask for help when you need it, and maintain reciprocal relationships that advance everyone's goals. But don't confuse professional cooperation with personal loyalty.

Participate in social activities strategically. Attend enough events to stay connected and avoid being seen as antisocial, but don't become so central to office social dynamics that your professional reputation gets entangled with personal dramas. Keep one foot in and one foot out.

When conflicts arise, remember that you're dealing with colleagues, not friends. Don't expect personal loyalty to override professional incentives. Don't take professional competition personally. Don't let workplace conflicts affect your ability to work effectively with people, but don't pretend they're purely personal issues either.

Build your real social network outside of work. Invest in friendships and relationships that aren't complicated by professional competition, power dynamics, or conflicting interests. Having a strong personal support system makes you less dependent on workplace relationships for emotional fulfillment and social connection.

The professional network is different from the social network. Maintain relationships with former colleagues, industry contacts, and professional acquaintances who can provide career opportunities, references, and industry intelligence. These relationships are explicitly transactional, which makes them more honest and often more durable than work friendships.

Exercises

Audit your current workplace relationships honestly. Which relationships are based on genuine compatibility versus shared circumstances? Which colleagues do you trust with sensitive information, and why? Are those relationships symmetrical, or are you sharing more than you're receiving?

Create information boundaries that protect your professional interests. What topics will you avoid discussing with coworkers? How will you redirect conversations that get too personal or too revealing? What information do you need to keep confidential to protect your career strategies?

Develop responses to common workplace social situations that maintain professional boundaries without seeming antisocial. How will you handle invitations to complain about management? How will you participate in office gossip without contributing damaging information? How will you maintain relationships without creating obligations?

Build a support network outside of work that can provide the emotional connection and social fulfillment you might otherwise seek from colleagues. Who are the people in your life who can provide advice, support, and friendship without any professional conflicts of interest?

Practice separating professional cooperation from personal friendship. Can you work effectively with people you don't like? Can you maintain professional relationships with people who've disappointed you personally? Can you compete for opportunities with people you genuinely care about?

Understanding that workplace relationships are transactional doesn't make them less valuable. It makes them more honest. Stop expecting unconditional loyalty from people whose professional obligations conflict with yours, and you can appreciate what they do provide without being blindsided when their priorities shift.

The best workplace relationships are the ones where everyone understands the rules and plays fairly within them. Professional respect, mutual benefit, and appropriate boundaries create better working relationships than false intimacy and unrealistic expectations.

Your coworkers aren't your friends, and that's liberating. It means you can focus on being good at your job instead of managing complex social dynamics. It means you can make career decisions based on your interests instead of feeling obligated to people who would do the same. It means you can be professional, effective, and successful without the emotional drama that comes from mixing personal and professional relationships.

Work is work. Keep it that way.

Toxic Colleague Countermeasures

The Problem

Toxic colleagues are like workplace cancer. They spread negativity, sabotage projects, steal credit, and create drama that makes everyone's job harder. The worst part is that they're often protected by management either because they're high performers in other areas, because they're skilled at managing up, or because dealing with them requires more effort than management wants to invest.

You can't fire your toxic colleagues, you can't avoid them completely, and you can't appeal to their better nature because they don't have one. But you're not powerless. Toxic people succeed because they exploit the assumption that everyone else will play by normal social rules while they break those rules for their advantage. Once you understand their tactics and develop countermeasures, you can neutralize their impact and sometimes even turn their toxicity against them.

The key is understanding that toxic colleagues aren't just difficult people having bad days. They're predators who deliberately target people they perceive as vulnerable, steal credit for work they didn't do, and create chaos that benefits them while harming everyone else. Treating them like reasonable people who can be managed through normal workplace relationships is like bringing a butter knife to a gunfight.

Discussion

Let's start with the credit thief, probably the most common and dangerous toxic colleague you'll encounter. They don't have original ideas, they don't do the hard work, but they're experts at positioning themselves to take credit for other people's successes. They'll volunteer to "help" with your project, then gradually take over the narrative until it becomes their project that you assisted with.

Credit thieves are masters of strategic visibility. They make sure they're present when successes are announced but mysteriously absent when problems need solving. They send emails to senior management "summarizing" team accomplishments that subtly position them as the leader. They volunteer to present your work to executives because they're "good at presentations," then gradually erase your contributions from the story.

The workplace bully operates differently but just as destructively. They use intimidation, public humiliation, and psychological warfare to control people and situations. They'll interrupt you in meetings, dismiss your ideas without consideration, and make condescending comments disguised as helpful feedback. They create an atmosphere of fear where people avoid challenging them or competing with them.

Bullies target people they perceive as threats or easy victims. If you're competent but non-confrontational, you're a perfect target because you have something they want (skills, recognition, opportunities) but you're unlikely to fight back effectively. They'll chip away at your confidence and reputation until you either leave or become so demoralized that you're no longer a threat.

The saboteur is perhaps the most dangerous because their damage is often invisible until it's too late. They'll withhold critical information, "forget" to include you in important meetings, provide misleading guidance that makes you look incompetent, and create obstacles that appear to be circumstances instead of deliberate interference.

Saboteurs are experts at plausible deniability. When your project fails because they didn't provide the data you needed, it looks like your planning failure, not their sabotage. When you miss an important deadline because they didn't tell you about a changed requirement, it appears to be your communication problem, not their deliberate withholding of information.

The gossip spreader uses information as a weapon to build alliances and destroy reputations. They collect secrets, spread rumors, and manipulate social dynamics to maintain power and influence. They'll be your best friend when they want information from you and your worst enemy when spreading that information serves their purposes.

Gossips create divisions within teams by sharing selective information that creates mistrust and conflict. They'll tell you what someone said about you (often exaggerated or taken out of context) to create drama and position themselves as your ally and information source. They thrive on chaos and interpersonal conflict because it gives them power and relevance.

The drama creator is addicted to crisis and controversy because it keeps them at the center of attention. They'll escalate minor disagreements into major conflicts, create problems that require their intervention to solve, and turn every workplace interaction into a soap opera where they're the star.

Drama creators are exhausting to deal with because they make everything about emotions, personalities, and relationships instead of work and results. They'll turn a simple project discussion into a referendum on who respects whom and who's being treated fairly. They make it impossible to have rational, productive conversations about work.

Solutions

The first rule of dealing with toxic colleagues is documentation. Everything. Every interaction, every email, every meeting, every commitment. Toxic people succeed because they rewrite history and gaslight their victims. Comprehensive documentation creates an objective record that can't be manipulated.

For credit thieves, the key is creating undeniable evidence of your contributions before they can steal them. Send emails outlining your ideas and approaches. Copy relevant stakeholders on project updates that detail your contributions. Volunteer to present your own work whenever possible. Create artifacts (documents, presentations, prototypes) that clearly show your authorship.

When credit thieves try to take over your narrative, correct the record immediately and publicly. "Thanks for presenting my analysis, Kieran. I'm happy to answer any technical questions about the methodology I developed." Don't be subtle or polite. Make your contributions visible and undeniable.

For workplace bullies, the counterstrategy is public professionalism combined with private documentation. Never respond to bullying behavior emotionally or defensively in public. Stay calm, professional, and focused on facts. But document every incident with dates, witnesses, and behaviors.

When a bully interrupts you in a meeting, say "I wasn't finished with my point" and continue. When they dismiss your ideas, ask "What concerns do you have with this approach?" Force them to be substantive instead of dismissive. Make them defend their behavior in front of witnesses.

Bullies rely on their targets being isolated and unsupported. Build alliances with colleagues who can serve as witnesses and advocates. Make sure other people see your competence and professionalism so the bully's narrative about your inadequacy doesn't stick.

For saboteurs, the defense is redundancy and verification. Never rely on a single source for critical information. Confirm important details through multiple channels. Follow up on commitments with written confirmation. Create backup plans for when promised resources or support don't materialize.

When sabotage occurs, document the impact and escalate immediately. "The project timeline we discussed is no longer feasible because the data promised for Monday wasn't delivered until Friday. How should we adjust expectations?" Make the sabotage visible and costly for the saboteur.

For gossips and drama creators, the strategy is information discipline and emotional neutrality. Don't provide them with ammunition by sharing personal information, complaints about management, or concerns about colleagues. When they try to create drama, redirect the conversation to work and facts.

"I don't discuss personnel issues, but I'm happy to talk about the project requirements." "I prefer to address concerns directly with the people involved instead of speculating about motivations." "Let's focus on what we need to accomplish instead of who said what to whom."

The nuclear option for dealing with toxic colleagues is strategic professional destruction. This should only be used when someone is deliberately damaging your career and normal countermeasures aren't working. The goal is to make their toxicity so visible and costly that management has no choice but to address it.

Build an airtight paper trail, create alliances with credible witnesses, and create situations where their toxic behavior is displayed in front of decision makers. Volunteer to work on high-visibility projects with them where their sabotage will be obvious to senior management. Let them destroy themselves through their own behavior while you maintain perfect professionalism.

Exercises

Identify the toxic colleagues in your workplace and categorize their behaviors. What tactics do they use? What triggers their toxic behavior? Who are their targets and allies? Understanding their patterns helps you develop targeted countermeasures.

Create a documentation system that captures interactions with toxic colleagues without being obvious about it. How will you record incidents? How will you store evidence securely? What information do you need to build a credible case if escalation becomes necessary?

Build strategic alliances with colleagues who can serve as witnesses and advocates. Who has influence with management? Who has credibility and good judgment? Who shares your interest in maintaining professional working relationships? These relationships become crucial when dealing with toxic behavior.

Develop response scripts for common toxic behaviors so you're prepared when they occur. How will you handle credit theft attempts? How will you respond to bullying behavior? How will you redirect gossip and drama? Having prepared responses prevents you from being caught off guard.

Practice emotional regulation techniques that help you stay professional when dealing with toxic behavior. What strategies help you remain calm under pressure? How can you respond to provocations without escalating conflicts? How can you maintain your credibility while protecting yourself?

Toxic colleagues succeed when good people do nothing. Your silence and accommodation enable their behavior. Protecting yourself isn't just good for you, it's good for everyone else who has to work with them.

The goal isn't to become toxic yourself. The goal is to neutralize toxicity through professional countermeasures that expose destructive behavior and protect productive people. Sometimes the best way to deal with workplace predators is to make it clear that you're not prey.

Don't let toxic people make you hate your job. Make them regret targeting you.

Remote and Hybrid Work Optimization

"The future of work is not about replacing humans with machines; it's about humans working with machines." - Ginni Rometty

---

The Problem

Remote work was supposed to be liberation from office politics, commutes, and micromanagement. Instead, many people discovered that working from home just means being monitored by different technology while sitting in uncomfortable chairs at kitchen tables, trying to look professional while their life falls apart in the background.

Companies sold remote work as a benefit while quietly implementing surveillance systems that would make an authoritarian regime jealous. They track your keystrokes, monitor your screen time, analyze your productivity metrics, and measure your engagement levels. You traded the freedom of leaving the office for the prison of never really leaving work because work now lives in your house.

The worst part is that most people are terrible at remote work because they're trying to replicate office dynamics in their living room instead of optimizing for the unique advantages and challenges of distributed work. You're not just competing against your colleagues anymore, you're competing against their carefully curated digital personas while your life intrudes on every video call.

Discussion

Let's start with the brutal truth about home offices. That inspiring Pinterest board of perfectly organized workspaces with plants, natural light, and minimalist aesthetics? Pure fantasy for most people. Your home office is probably a corner of your bedroom, a spot at the kitchen table, or a repurposed closet where you try to look professional while your family, pets, and neighbors create chaos in the background.

The lighting is terrible because residential spaces aren't designed for video calls. You look like you're being interrogated under fluorescent bulbs or like you're calling from a cave. Your internet cuts out during important presentations. Your neighbor decides to renovate their deck during your quarterly review. Your cat walks across your keyboard while you're sharing confidential financial data with the entire company.

Companies love talking about work-life balance while implementing systems that make it impossible to achieve. Slack notifications at 11 PM. "Quick questions" via text message on weekends. Video calls scheduled during lunch because someone in a different time zone wants to "sync up." Your home becomes an extension of the office, not a refuge from it.

The surveillance theater is insidious because it's disguised as productivity optimization. Employee monitoring software tracks everything: how many minutes you're active, how many applications you're using, how many emails you send, how long you spend in meetings. The data gets compiled into productivity scores that supposedly measure your contribution but measure your compliance with arbitrary activity metrics.

Some companies require employees to keep cameras on all day, turning remote work into a performance art piece where you have to maintain professional facial expressions while dealing with personal emergencies. Others use keystroke monitoring that flags you as unproductive if you spend too much time thinking instead of typing. The technology exists to help you work better, but it's being used to monitor whether you're working at all.

The digital presence game is exhausting because it requires constant performance management. You need to look engaged during video calls while mentally checking out of pointless meetings. You need to respond to messages quickly enough to seem available but not so quickly that people think you're not busy with important work. You need to participate in virtual team-building activities that are just as awkward as in-person team-building but now with technical difficulties.

Isolation is the hidden cost that nobody talks about during the remote work transition. Human beings are social creatures who need casual interaction, nonverbal communication, and spontaneous collaboration. Remote work strips away most of these elements and replaces them with scheduled video calls and Slack threads that feel artificial and exhausting.

The commute wasn't just travel time, it was transition time that helped you mentally shift between work mode and personal mode. When your office is your bedroom, that transition disappears. You roll out of bed and start checking emails. You finish work and immediately start thinking about personal tasks. The boundaries blur until everything feels like work and nothing feels like rest.

Technical failures become career disasters when you're entirely dependent on technology for professional interaction. Your internet crashes during the investor presentation. Your laptop dies in the middle of a client call. Your video feed freezes while you're making an important point, and everyone sees a screenshot of you mid-sneeze for the next five minutes.

The hybrid model creates new problems by combining the worst aspects of remote and office work. You're expected to be equally productive at home and in the office while adapting to completely different work environments. You miss important conversations because they happen in person on days you're working remotely. You're excluded from spontaneous collaborations because half the team is distributed and can't participate in real-time.

Solutions

Winning at remote work means treating it as a completely different skill set that requires intentional optimization, not just adapting your office behavior to your living room. You need to engineer your environment, master the technology, and game the surveillance systems while building the isolation mitigation strategies you need to stay sane.

Start by creating a dedicated workspace that works for your life, not an Instagram fantasy. If you can't have a separate room, create visual and psychological boundaries that help you transition between work and personal time. Invest in lighting that makes you look competent on video calls. Get noise-cancelling headphones that let you focus despite household chaos.

Your camera angle should be at eye level, not looking up your nose or down at your forehead. Position yourself with a neutral background or use a virtual background that doesn't glitch when you move. Test your audio quality because people will tolerate bad video but they won't tolerate bad audio. Have backup internet options because technical difficulties stop being cute after the first few incidents.

Master the productivity theater that surveillance systems reward. Keep multiple applications open to appear busy. Move your mouse occasionally if you're reading or thinking. Schedule emails to send during business hours even if you write them at weird times. Learn what activities generate the metrics your company values and optimize for those signals instead of productivity.

Most employee monitoring systems measure activity, not output. If your company tracks keystrokes, spend time writing detailed project documentation that adds value while generating impressive activity metrics. If they track screen time, keep work applications open while you're thinking through problems. Game the system by understanding what it measures and giving it what it wants.

Build strategies to fight isolation that don't depend on company initiatives. Schedule regular video coffee breaks with colleagues you like. Join professional groups that provide intellectual stimulation and career networking. Create accountability partnerships with other remote workers who understand the unique challenges. Maintain friendships outside of work that provide social connection without professional competition.

The goal isn't to replicate office socialization at home, it's to create better socialization that serves your needs instead of your company's needs. You have more control over your social interactions when you're not trapped in an office with people you didn't choose to spend time with.

Prepare for technical failures like a professional. Have backup internet through your phone's hotspot. Know how to quickly join calls from your mobile device. Keep important presentations saved locally in case cloud services fail. Practice transitioning between devices so technical problems become minor inconveniences instead of career disasters.

When technical issues occur, acknowledge them briefly and move on. "Sorry, my connection dropped for a moment. As I was saying..." Don't apologize excessively or explain your home internet situation. Handle glitches professionally and people will remember your recovery more than the problem.

Remote work gives you advantages that office workers don't have if you're strategic about using them. You can control your environment completely. You can optimize your schedule for your natural energy patterns. You can eliminate commute time and use it for activities that improve your life. You can work from anywhere with internet, giving you geographic flexibility that traditional employees don't have.

Exercises

Audit your current home office setup for both productivity and professional appearance. What improvements would have the biggest impact on your ability to work effectively? What changes would make you look more competent during video calls? What investments in equipment or furniture would pay for themselves through improved performance?

Test all your technology systems under stress conditions. What happens when your primary internet connection fails? How quickly can you transition to backup systems? What are your weak points that could cause professional embarrassment? Create redundancy for critical systems so failures don't become disasters.

Develop your own approach to staying connected that doesn't rely on company-provided social interaction. What professional groups could you join? What colleagues could you build deeper relationships with outside of official work activities? What non-work social connections do you need to maintain your mental health?

Create a remote work bingo card for your own entertainment. "Internet cuts out during important presentation." "Pet interrupts video call." "Forgot to mute while eating." "Virtual background fails at crucial moment." Having a sense of humor about remote work disasters makes them less stressful when they inevitably occur.

Build your digital presence management skills so you can control how you're perceived in virtual interactions. Practice your on-camera persona. Learn to use technology smoothly and professionally. Develop techniques for staying engaged during boring video calls without looking bored.

Remote work is a skill that requires intentional development, not just a location change. Treat it as a completely different way of working with its own strategies and rules.

Companies will continue trying to recreate office culture virtually, but you don't have to participate in that charade. You can build a remote work experience that serves your needs while meeting their requirements. Use the flexibility of remote work to create better working conditions for yourself, not to accept worse ones just because you're at home.

Remote work done right is better than office work. Remote work done wrong is a prison that follows you everywhere you go. Make sure you're building the right version.

Why We Stay in Jobs We Hate

"The cave you fear to enter holds the treasure you seek." -
Joseph Campbell

The Problem

You know your job is slowly destroying your soul, but you stay anyway. You complain about it constantly, fantasize about quitting dramatically, and scroll through job postings during lunch breaks, but somehow you never take action. You've convinced yourself that you're trapped by circumstances beyond your control when the real trap is psychological conditioning designed to keep you compliant and afraid.

The prison isn't made of walls and bars, it's made of fear, convenience, and learned helplessness. Companies have figured out how to create just enough comfort to prevent you from leaving while providing just enough misery to keep you desperate for their approval. They've weaponized your insecurities, your financial obligations, and your social conditioning to create a workforce that's too scared to leave and too beaten down to demand better treatment.

What makes this trap so hard to escape is how they've convinced you that your fear is rational and your alternatives are limited. Every doubt you have about leaving, every worry about finding something better, every concern about starting over has been carefully cultivated by systems designed to make you feel powerless. Breaking free isn't just about finding a new job, it's about recognizing and dismantling the psychological control mechanisms that keep you trapped.

Discussion

I know this chapter from the inside. Early in my career I stayed at jobs that had become genuinely miserable — not difficult, not imperfect, but hell — because I was living paycheck to paycheck and my bosses were skilled at making me believe I had it lucky. No one else would hire me, they said. Certainly not at my salary level. They'd reward me later. All of it was lies, but I had no financial cushion to test whether the threats were real, so they stayed credible.

I didn't leave until I was effectively forced out. In one job the company payroll started becoming unreliable — which is a polite way of saying I stopped being able to count on being paid. In another, a peer manager decided to make my life his personal project, undermining me and screaming at me every single day until the situation was untenable. Both times I found something new before I walked out the door.

That detail matters: I waited until the alternative existed. That's not strength, that's what fear looks like in practice. If I'd had a financial buffer and understood how replaceable my bosses' threats were, I'd have left on my own terms, months earlier, from a position of choice instead of necessity. That's what this chapter is about.

Let's start with the foundation of workplace psychological control: fear. Companies don't just want your labor, they want your desperation. A desperate employee is a compliant employee. Someone who's afraid of losing their job will accept longer hours, lower pay, poor treatment, and unreasonable demands without pushing back. Fear makes you grateful for scraps instead of demanding fair compensation.

The "you're lucky to have a job" gaslighting is perhaps the most effective control mechanism in corporate America. Every time you consider asking for a raise, pushing back on unreasonable demands, or looking for better opportunities, that voice kicks in: "At least you have a job. People are unemployed. The economy is uncertain. You should be grateful." This narrative transforms employment from a mutual exchange of value into a gift that can be revoked if you're not sufficiently appreciative.

Financial fear is the golden handcuffs that keep talented people trapped in terrible situations. The mortgage, the car payments, the credit card debt, the kids' college fund. Every financial obligation becomes a reason why you can't afford to take risks or make changes. Companies love employees with high fixed expenses because they're predictable and controllable. Someone with six months of savings and minimal debt can walk away from a toxic situation. Someone living paycheck to paycheck has to endure whatever treatment they receive.

Health insurance has become the ultimate trap for American workers. The fear of losing coverage keeps people in jobs they hate because the alternative might be medical bankruptcy. Companies know this and use it strategically. They'll offer decent health benefits while providing terrible working conditions because they know most people won't risk their family's health for their personal happiness. The healthcare system has become a tool of employment control.

Imposter syndrome is systematically cultivated and exploited to keep talented people believing they're not qualified for better opportunities. Companies love employees who think they're lucky to be there and wouldn't be successful anywhere else. They'll promote you just enough to make you feel like you've achieved something while constantly reminding you that your success is due to their investment in you, not your own capabilities.

The sunk cost fallacy keeps people trapped in situations they would never choose to enter. "I've been here for eight years. I can't throw that away." "I'm two years from being vested in the pension plan." "I've built relationships here that would be hard to replace." The longer you stay, the harder it becomes to leave because you start viewing your past investment as a reason to continue instead of a lesson learned.

Age discrimination fears are powerful because they're based on real workplace bias. Companies love making older employees feel like they're unemployable elsewhere while simultaneously treating them as expensive and outdated. The message is clear: you're too old to start over but too expensive to keep unless you accept whatever conditions we offer. This creates a workforce of experienced people who stay in bad situations because they believe their options are limited.

Social pressure compounds the internal fears with external expectations. Family members who think any job is better than no job. Friends who can't understand why you'd leave a "good job" for something uncertain. Society's message that job-hopping is irresponsible and loyalty is virtuous. The social safety net depends on employment, so leaving a job feels like failing your obligations to everyone who depends on you.

The comfort zone trap is insidious because it disguises stagnation as stability. You know your current job, understand the politics, have established routines, and can perform your duties without much effort. Starting over somewhere new requires energy, learning, and emotional investment that feels overwhelming when you're already exhausted by your current situation. Better the devil you know than the devil you don't.

Economic terrorism is how companies use broader economic conditions to justify poor treatment. During recessions, they cut benefits and freeze salaries while reminding employees how lucky they are to have jobs. During growth periods, they increase demands and expectations while claiming they can't afford competitive compensation because they need to invest in the business. There's never a good time to ask for more or expect better treatment.

The "golden handcuffs" narrative is designed to make you feel like you're receiving special treatment that would be impossible to find elsewhere. Stock options that vest in five years, retention bonuses that require long-term commitments, retirement benefits that only pay out after decades of service. These aren't generous benefits, they're control mechanisms designed to make leaving expensive and psychologically difficult.

Solutions

Breaking free from a job you hate requires dismantling each psychological control mechanism systematically while building the confidence and resources you need to create better options. The goal isn't to quit impulsively, it's to eliminate the fears that keep you trapped so you can make decisions from strength instead of desperation.

Start by building financial independence that gives you options. Live below your means, pay down debt aggressively, and build an emergency fund that can support you for at least six months without income. Every dollar you save is a vote for your future freedom. Financial independence doesn't mean you're rich, it means you're not desperate.

Challenge the "you're lucky to have a job" narrative by understanding your market value. Research salaries for your role in your market. Talk to recruiters about opportunities. Network with people in your field to understand what's available. The job market is almost always better than companies want you to believe, and your options are almost always broader than you think.

Address imposter syndrome by documenting your achievements and building confidence in your capabilities. Keep a record of problems you've solved, value you've created, and skills you've developed. Get feedback from colleagues, clients, and industry contacts who can provide objective perspective on your competence and potential. You're probably much more qualified and capable than you realize.

Break the sunk cost fallacy by focusing on future opportunity cost instead of past investment. The question isn't "How much have I invested in this job?" but "What opportunities am I missing by staying?" The years you've spent building someone else's business could have been spent building your own career. Don't let past investment trap you in future misery.

Address age discrimination fears by building skills and networks that make you valuable regardless of your age. The people who struggle with age discrimination are often the ones who stopped learning, growing, and adapting. Stay current with industry trends, develop new capabilities, and maintain relationships that can provide opportunities. Age becomes an advantage when it's combined with continued growth and learning.

Handle social pressure by educating the people who matter about your situation and goals. Help family members understand that staying in a job that makes you miserable isn't responsible, it's self-destructive. Build relationships with people who support your growth instead of your compliance. Surround yourself with people who encourage you to take intelligent risks instead of accepting mediocre certainty.

Expand your comfort zone gradually by taking on new challenges while still employed. Volunteer for projects outside your normal responsibilities. Learn new skills that could transfer to other roles or industries. Build relationships with people outside your current company. The goal is to prove to yourself that you can handle change and uncertainty successfully.

Counter economic terrorism by understanding that economic conditions affect everyone, not just you. Companies that treat employees poorly during tough times will continue treating them poorly during good times. Economic uncertainty is a constant, not an exception. The question isn't whether there will be challenges, but whether you want to face those challenges from a position of strength or weakness.

Evaluate "golden handcuffs" honestly by calculating their real value versus the opportunity cost of staying. Stock options in a mediocre company might be worth less than higher base salary somewhere else. Retention bonuses that require multi-year commitments might cost you more in lost opportunities than they provide in guaranteed payments. Retirement benefits that vest in the distant future might not compensate for years of career stagnation.

Exercises

Conduct a fear inventory to identify which psychological control mechanisms are keeping you trapped. What worries you most about leaving your job? Which of these fears are based on evidence versus assumptions and social conditioning? What would you need to address each fear systematically?

Calculate your real financial runway and create a plan to extend it. How long could you survive without income? What expenses could you cut if necessary? What debts could you pay off to reduce your fixed obligations? How much money would give you the confidence to make a career change?

Research your market value and opportunities thoroughly. What are people in similar roles earning at other companies? What skills are in demand in your field? What companies are hiring people with your background? What would you need to learn or change to access better opportunities?

Build confidence systematically by documenting your achievements and getting external validation. What problems have you solved that others couldn't? What value have you created that's measurable? What feedback have you received that confirms your competence? Who outside your current company could vouch for your capabilities?

Create a transition plan that reduces risk while building alternatives. What skills could you develop while still employed? What relationships could you build? What opportunities could you explore? How could you test new directions without jeopardizing your current situation?

The psychological prison is real, but it's not permanent. Every fear that keeps you trapped can be addressed through preparation, planning, and confidence built one decision at a time. You don't have to choose between security and happiness. You can build the skills, resources, and relationships that make better opportunities possible.

You're not trying to become reckless or impulsive. You're trying to eliminate the fears that prevent you from making rational decisions. When you're no longer afraid of change, you can choose your circumstances instead of accepting whatever circumstances choose you.

Your job should serve your life, not consume it. If it's doing the latter, you have more power to change the situation than you realize. The question isn't whether you can afford to leave, it's whether you can afford to stay.

HR Is Not Your Friend (Critical Intel)

"HR is like a pimp. They're paid to keep you happy enough to keep working, but not so happy that you realize you deserve better." – Anonymous

---

The Problem

HR has successfully rebranded itself as the employee advocate, the workplace counselor, and the guardian of company culture. They've convinced people that they exist to solve employee problems, mediate conflicts, and ensure fair treatment. This is perhaps the most dangerous lie in corporate America because it leads employees to trust the very department designed to protect the company from them.

HR's primary function is legal and financial risk mitigation. Every policy they create, every procedure they implement, and every interaction they have with employees is designed to minimize the company's liability and maximize their legal defensibility. When HR says they want to help you with a problem, what they really mean is they want to assess whether your problem poses a threat to the company and, if so, eliminate that threat as efficiently as possible.

The "people first" marketing is brilliant because it makes employees voluntarily provide the information HR needs to protect the company against them. You walk into their office thinking you're getting help, and you walk out having created a documented record of your complaints that can be used to justify whatever action the company wants to take against you.

Discussion

Let's start with what HR does versus what they claim to do. They claim to be employee advocates who ensure fair treatment and positive workplace culture. What they do is create policies that protect the company from lawsuits, document employee behavior to justify termination decisions, and manage the process of hiring and firing people in legally defensible ways.

Every HR policy is written by lawyers to create maximum legal protection for the company. The employee handbook isn't a guide to your rights, it's a document that limits your rights and establishes the company's legal defenses. When you sign it, you're not agreeing to be treated fairly, you're agreeing to accept whatever treatment the company can justify under the policies you just acknowledged receiving.

The open-door policy is a trap disguised as accessibility. They want you to come to them with problems because it creates a documented record of your complaints and gives them the opportunity to control the narrative. When you report harassment, discrimination, or illegal behavior, the first thing HR does is assess whether addressing your complaint serves the company's interests. If it does, they'll act. If it doesn't, they'll find reasons why your complaint isn't valid or actionable.

HR investigations are designed to protect the company, not uncover the truth. They interview witnesses to gather information that supports their predetermined conclusion. They document everything in ways that minimize legal liability. They focus on policy violations instead of ethical violations because policies are legally defensible. The goal isn't justice, it's legal insulation.

The performance improvement plan is HR's favorite weapon because it creates a documented path to termination that appears fair and objective. PIPs are rarely designed to help employees improve, they're designed to create evidence that the employee was given opportunities to improve and failed to meet clearly defined expectations. The metrics are often impossible to achieve or subjectively measured, giving managers the flexibility to justify whatever outcome they want.

Harassment and discrimination complaints are handled through a carefully choreographed process designed to minimize legal exposure. HR will investigate just enough to claim they took the complaint seriously, but not enough to uncover systemic problems that could expose the company to larger liability. They'll often conclude that the behavior, while inappropriate, doesn't rise to the level of illegal harassment, allowing them to avoid taking meaningful action while creating documentation that they addressed the issue.

The exit interview is HR's final intelligence-gathering operation. They want to know why you're leaving, what problems you encountered, and whether you might pose any legal threats after departure. The information you provide helps them assess legal risks and prepare defenses against potential claims. Your honest feedback about toxic managers or illegal practices gets filed away to protect the company, not to fix the problems.

Employee engagement surveys are another data collection exercise disguised as employee advocacy. The questions are designed to measure legal risk factors: Are people likely to quit? Are there harassment issues we need to address? Are there pay equity problems that could become lawsuits? The results are used to manage risks, not improve working conditions.

The "culture fit" assessment is how HR legally discriminates against people they don't want to hire or keep. Culture fit can mean anything: too old, too expensive, too likely to ask uncomfortable questions, too willing to report problems. It's a subjective standard that can justify almost any hiring or firing decision while providing legal cover against discrimination claims.

Mediation and conflict resolution services exist to prevent employee disputes from becoming legal problems. HR doesn't care whether conflicts are resolved fairly, they care whether they're resolved in ways that minimize legal exposure. The mediator's job is to get employees to accept solutions that protect the company, not solutions that address the underlying problems.

The "business partner" model is insidious because it makes clear where HR's loyalties lie. They're partners with management, not advocates for employees. Their job is to help managers achieve business objectives while minimizing legal risks. When employee interests conflict with business interests, guess which side HR supports?

Confidentiality promises are selectively enforced based on what serves the company's interests. They'll keep your complaints confidential if revealing them would create legal liability. They'll share your personal information with management if it helps them address potential problems. The confidentiality flows one way: they can share anything about you that serves business purposes, but you can't share anything about them that doesn't.

Solutions

The key to dealing with HR is understanding their true function and interacting with them accordingly. You're not talking to a counselor or advocate, you're talking to the company's legal defense team. Everything you say can and will be used to protect the company's interests, not yours.

Never go to HR with a problem unless you're prepared for the consequences of creating a documented record of that problem. If you complain about harassment, be prepared for retaliation disguised as performance management. If you report illegal behavior, be prepared to become the problem employee who creates drama. If you express dissatisfaction with company policies, be prepared to be labeled as not a culture fit.

When you do need to interact with HR, control the information flow carefully. Stick to facts, avoid emotional language, and focus on behavior instead of intentions. Don't speculate about motivations or share personal information that could be used against you. Get everything in writing and keep copies of all documentation.

If you have a legitimate legal complaint, bypass HR and go directly to a lawyer. HR's job is to prevent legal claims, not facilitate them. They'll often try to resolve issues internally in ways that protect the company while preventing you from pursuing legal remedies. Don't let them control the process if you have genuine legal rights at stake.

Document everything yourself before involving HR. Keep records of incidents, save emails, and gather evidence independently. HR investigations are designed to create the minimum documentation necessary to justify their preferred outcome. Your independent documentation might be the only objective record of what happened.

Understand that HR policies are minimum legal requirements, not employee rights. Just because something violates company policy doesn't mean it's illegal. Just because something is allowed by company policy doesn't mean it's appropriate. Focus on legal violations instead of policy violations if you want external recourse.

Build relationships with employment lawyers before you need them. Know your rights under federal and state employment laws. Understand the difference between illegal behavior and merely unfair behavior. Know what documentation you need to support different types of claims. Don't rely on HR to educate you about your legal rights.

When dealing with performance issues, get feedback in writing and respond in writing. Don't accept vague criticism or subjective evaluations. Ask for examples, measurable goals, and clear timelines. Create your own documentation of your performance and achievements that can counter their narrative if necessary.

If you're terminated, don't sign anything immediately. Review severance agreements with an employment lawyer before accepting them. Understand what rights you're waiving and what protections you're giving up. Negotiate terms that serve your interests, not just the company's interests.

Review your company's employee handbook and policies with a critical eye. What rights are you guaranteed versus what protections the company has created for itself? What procedures favor the company's interests over employee interests? What language creates ambiguity that could be interpreted against employees?

Audit your past interactions with HR to understand how information you shared might have been used. What complaints or concerns did you raise? How were they handled? What documentation was created? How might that information be used if you ever have conflicts with the company?

Research your state's employment laws to understand your legal rights versus your company policy rights. What behavior is illegal versus merely inappropriate? What documentation would you need to support different types of legal claims? What agencies could investigate violations of employment law?

Create a strategy for documenting workplace issues that protects your interests. What incidents should you record? How will you store documentation securely? What evidence do you need to support potential legal claims? How will you document your own performance and achievements?

Develop relationships with employment lawyers in your area who could advise you if needed. What employment law issues do they handle? What do they charge for consultations? What documentation do they recommend employees maintain? How do they evaluate potential employment law claims?

HR exists to protect the company from legal and financial liability, not to advocate for you. They're not evil people doing an evil job. They're people doing a job that requires them to put company interests first. Understanding that distinction keeps you from being caught off guard.

The goal isn't to avoid HR entirely, it's to understand their role and limitations so you can protect yourself while still accessing the services you need. Use them when it serves your interests, avoid them when it doesn't, and never forget that their primary obligation is to the company that pays their salary, not to the employees who need their help.

Trust them as much as they trust you, which is to say, not at all.

Skills and Career Development - AI-Proof Your Future

"The illiterate of the 21st century will not be those who cannot read and write, but those who cannot learn, unlearn, and relearn." - Alvin Toffler

---

The Problem

The advice industry has convinced people that the solution to job insecurity is constant skill building, as if you can learn your way to permanent employment. They sell you expensive courses, certifications, and degree programs while the fundamental nature of work changes faster than any curriculum can adapt. Most "professional development" is just expensive procrastination disguised as career advancement.

Companies love employees who are obsessed with skill building because it shifts the responsibility for career security from the employer to the employee. Can't find a job? You must need more skills. Got laid off? Should have stayed current with technology. Struggling to get promoted? Time for another certification. It's a brilliant scam that makes you pay for training while they benefit from your improved capabilities.

The real challenge isn't learning new skills, it's developing the ability to adapt faster than technology can replace you. AI isn't just automating manual labor anymore, it's automating knowledge work, creative work, and decision-making processes. The question isn't which skills are AI-proof, it's how to position yourself as someone who makes AI more valuable instead of someone AI makes obsolete.

Discussion

Let's start with the brutal reality about skills gap analysis. Most of what companies claim they need is either outdated by the time you learn it or completely different from what they hire for. Job postings ask for five years of experience with technology that's been around for two years. They want specialists with generalist capabilities and generalists with specialist expertise. They demand creativity and compliance, innovation and risk aversion, leadership and followership.

The skills gap isn't really about skills, it's about companies wanting perfect employees at entry-level prices. They'd prefer to complain about talent shortages than pay market rates for the talent that exists. They post job requirements that describe unicorns and then act surprised when unicorns don't apply for their mediocre positions.

Professional development has become another form of employee exploitation. Companies encourage you to learn new skills on your own time, with your own money, for their benefit. They'll happily use your new capabilities while providing no guarantee that investing in those capabilities will result in advancement, higher pay, or job security. You bear the cost and risk of skill development while they reap the rewards.

The certification industrial complex preys on insecurity and promotes the myth that credentials equal competence. Microsoft, Google, Amazon, and other tech giants have created certification programs that train you to use their products while making you feel like you're building career security. These aren't neutral education programs, they're customer acquisition strategies disguised as professional development.

Most certifications are designed to generate revenue for the certifying organization, not to create meaningful skill differentiation for the people who earn them. When everyone has the same certifications, having that certification becomes the minimum requirement instead of a competitive advantage. You've paid money to achieve the baseline expectation.

Age discrimination in skills-based hiring is vicious because it disguises bias as merit. Companies will claim they need someone with "digital native" capabilities or "cutting-edge" expertise, when what they really want is someone young enough to work for less money and naive enough to accept poor treatment. They use skill requirements as legal cover for age discrimination.

The "learn to code" mythology has created a generation of people who think programming skills are a guaranteed path to career security. But coding is increasingly being automated by AI, and the market is flooded with people who learned basic programming skills without understanding software engineering, system design, or business problem-solving. Learning syntax is not the same as developing engineering judgment.

The constant pressure to stay current with rapidly changing technology creates a hamster wheel of learning that never leads to mastery or career advancement. You spend so much time learning new tools that you never develop deep expertise in anything. You become a perpetual beginner in multiple areas instead of an expert in domains that matter.

Self-directed learning has become another way to transfer training costs from employers to employees. Instead of providing professional development opportunities, companies expect you to figure out what you need to learn, find your own resources, and develop capabilities on your own time. Then they act like they're doing you a favor by giving you projects that use your self-funded education.

The speed of technological change means that most technical skills have shorter half-lives than the time it takes to become proficient in them. By the time you've mastered a technology, framework, or methodology, the industry has moved on to something else. You're constantly chasing a moving target while the rules of the game change around you.

Solutions

The key to AI-proofing your career isn't learning skills that won't be automated, it's developing meta-skills that make you valuable regardless of what technology can do. Focus on capabilities that complement AI instead of competing with it. Become the person who knows how to use AI tools effectively instead of someone who can be replaced by them.

Start with judgment and decision-making skills that require human context and experience. AI can process data and generate options, but humans need to evaluate those options based on organizational culture, political considerations, risk tolerance, and strategic priorities. Develop your ability to make good decisions with incomplete information under time pressure.

Communication and relationship-building skills become more valuable as work becomes more automated. When routine tasks are handled by AI, human work becomes more focused on collaboration, negotiation, persuasion, and conflict resolution. People who can work effectively with others, manage stakeholder relationships, and navigate organizational dynamics will always be in demand.

Problem identification and framing skills are more valuable than problem-solving skills. AI is getting very good at solving well-defined problems, but it's terrible at figuring out what the real problem is in messy, ambiguous situations. Develop your ability to understand what's broken, why it matters, and how it fits into larger systems and contexts.

They've spent years rewarding output while dismissing the people who could explain, translate, and manage it. That's exactly why emotional intelligence, communication, and judgment are where the compensation premium is moving now. The person who can translate what the engineering team built into something the board understands gets paid like an executive. Develop your ability to navigate complex human dynamics, make decisions under uncertainty, and handle the situations that don't have a clean algorithmic answer.

Learn to work with AI tools as augmentation instead of replacement. Become proficient with AI-assisted coding, writing, analysis, and design. The goal isn't to compete with AI, it's to use it for the grunt work and show up with judgment, context, and relationships it can't replicate. The people who master human-AI collaboration will have an advantage over those who ignore or fear the technology.

Build skills that span disciplines and industries instead of going deep in a single technical area. The most valuable people are often the ones who can bridge different domains, translate between technical and business stakeholders, and see connections that specialists miss. Develop T-shaped skills: broad knowledge across multiple areas with deep expertise in one or two domains.

Entrepreneurial skills matter more now than at any point in the last fifty years, because the social contract that made pure employment viable is dead. Learn to identify opportunities, validate ideas, build products, and find customers. You may never leave your day job — but understanding how businesses actually create value makes you harder to replace and better at knowing when you're being underpaid.

Teaching and mentoring are two of the most AI-resistant skills that exist, because they require reading the specific person in front of you and adjusting in real time. As information becomes essentially free, the ability to help someone actually use it becomes the scarce and valuable thing.

Financial literacy is the skill they never teach you in corporate training programs, and that's not an accident. The more you understand about money, investing, and building income outside your paycheck, the less trapped you are. Every point of financial independence is a point of negotiating leverage. Build it deliberately.

Exercises

Conduct an honest assessment of your current skills versus market demand. What capabilities do you have that are genuinely valuable and differentiated? What skills are you developing that might be automated soon? Where are the gaps between what you can do and what employers need?

Identify the meta-skills that underlie your technical capabilities. What judgment, experience, and intuition do you bring to your work that couldn't be replicated by following a process or algorithm? How can you articulate and develop these higher-level capabilities?

Experiment with AI tools in your current role to understand how they can augment your work. What tasks can be automated or accelerated? What new capabilities do AI tools give you? How can you use AI to focus on higher-value activities?

Build relationships with people in different industries and functions to understand how your skills might transfer to other domains. What problems do they face that your background could help solve? What opportunities exist that you might not be aware of?

Create a learning plan that balances depth and breadth. What domain should you go deep in to build genuine expertise? What adjacent areas should you learn enough about to communicate effectively with specialists? How will you stay current without falling into the hamster wheel of constant skill acquisition?

Don't waste energy trying to compete with software at software tasks. Focus on becoming exceptional at work that requires judgment, relationships, and accountability — the things AI can assist with but can't own. The people who win aren't the ones who learn every new tool. They're the ones who stay valuable regardless of which tools are in use.

Skills are important, but adaptability is more important. The ability to learn quickly, unlearn outdated approaches, and relearn new methods will serve you better than any technical capability. In a rapidly changing economy, your meta-learning skills are your most valuable asset.

The question isn't whether AI will change your industry. The question is whether you'll adapt faster than your competition. Start positioning yourself as someone who embraces change instead of someone who fears it. The future belongs to people who can evolve.

Compensation Warfare - Getting Paid What You're Worth

"If you don't value your time, neither will others. Stop giving away your time and talents. Value what you know & start charging for it." - Kim Garst

---

The Problem

Most people are terrible at getting paid what they're worth because they've been conditioned to be grateful for whatever they're offered and afraid to ask for more. Companies have created elaborate systems to keep salary information secret, make compensation discussions uncomfortable, and convince employees that their pay is fair when it's often substantially below market rate.

The compensation game is rigged against employees from the start. Companies have access to salary surveys, compensation consultants, and market data that employees don't see. They know exactly what they can get away with paying while maintaining the illusion that their offers are competitive. Meanwhile, you're supposed to negotiate blind, grateful for whatever scraps they throw your way.

The situation has gotten worse as companies have shifted from straightforward salary and benefits packages to complex compensation structures involving stock options, bonuses, equity grants, and other forms of payment that are difficult to evaluate and often worth far less than they appear. They've made compensation so complicated that most people have no idea whether they're getting a good deal or being systematically underpaid.

Discussion

Let's start with the fundamental lie of "competitive compensation." When companies say their salaries are competitive, they mean competitive with the lowest-paying companies in their market, not competitive with what good people can earn elsewhere. They use salary surveys that lag current market conditions by months or years, and they cherry-pick data that supports their preferred pay ranges.

The salary transparency movement has helped expose some of this manipulation, but companies have adapted by creating more complex job titles and compensation structures that make direct comparisons difficult. They'll call the same role different names at different companies, split responsibilities across multiple positions, or create custom job descriptions that don't match standard market categories.

Stock options have become the modern version of company scrip, the currency that mining companies used to pay workers that could only be spent at company stores. Companies offer equity that sounds valuable but comes with so many restrictions, vesting schedules, and performance requirements that it's often worthless. They use the theoretical value of unvested options to justify below-market salaries while the value to employees is zero until they can sell.

The benefits shell game is another way companies disguise poor compensation. They'll offer expensive-sounding benefits packages that are worth less than cash. Health insurance with high deductibles, retirement plans with poor investment options, PTO policies that discourage taking time off, and perks that benefit the company more than the employee.

Performance-based compensation is designed to shift risk from the company to the employee while giving the company maximum flexibility to reduce pay when convenient. Bonuses tied to company performance, individual metrics, or subjective evaluations can disappear during difficult years while base salaries remain suppressed. You bear the downside risk while the company controls the upside potential.

The annual review process is structured to minimize salary increases by making them feel like generous gifts instead of market adjustments. They'll give you a 3% increase when inflation is 5% and act like they're rewarding your excellent performance. They compare your raise to what other employees received instead of what you could earn elsewhere.

Negotiation intimidation is systematic and deliberate. They'll make you feel like asking for more money is greedy, unprofessional, or risky. They'll claim budget constraints while executives receive massive compensation packages. They'll suggest that non-monetary benefits should compensate for below-market pay. They want you to feel guilty for advocating for yourself.

The "we don't negotiate" lie is used to prevent salary discussions while protecting companies from having to justify their low offers. They'll claim that fairness requires giving everyone the same offer, ignoring the fact that market rates vary based on experience, skills, and performance. Some people are worth more than others, and pretending otherwise is just a way to pay everyone less.

Geographic pay adjustments have become another tool for reducing compensation while maintaining the appearance of fairness. Companies will pay different amounts based on where you live, supposedly reflecting local cost of living, but the adjustments rarely reflect market conditions. They'll use geography as an excuse to pay remote workers less while expecting the same productivity and availability.

The total compensation con involves adding up salary, benefits, perks, and theoretical equity value to create an impressive-looking package that obscures the fact that the cash compensation is below market. They'll include employer tax contributions, office amenities, and training opportunities in the total to inflate the apparent value while most of these "benefits" cost them nothing to provide.

Solutions

Winning the compensation game requires preparation, information, and strategic thinking. You need to understand your market value, document your contributions, and negotiate from a position of strength instead of desperation. The goal isn't to get rich from your employer, it's to get paid fairly for the value you create.

Start by researching your market value using multiple sources and current data. Salary websites give you baseline information, but recruiting conversations give you real-world market intelligence. Talk to recruiters even when you're not looking for a job. Network with people in similar roles at other companies. Ask direct questions about compensation ranges during informational interviews.

Track your contributions in concrete, quantifiable terms so you can make a real case for higher compensation. Document the problems you've solved, the value you've created, the costs you've saved, and the revenue you've generated. Business impact is the only argument that matters in compensation discussions. Everything else is just emotional manipulation.

Understand the total compensation package and evaluate each component separately. What's the base salary compared to market rates? What are the benefits worth in cash terms? What's the realistic value of equity compensation? What are the vesting schedules and performance requirements? Don't let them bundle everything together to obscure the value.

Time your compensation discussions strategically around performance reviews, project completions, and budget planning cycles. Don't ask for raises randomly or when the company is struggling. Build your case during times when your value is most visible and the company has the most flexibility to respond positively.

Negotiate everything, not just base salary. Vacation time, flexible work arrangements, professional development budgets, equipment allowances, and title changes can all add value to your package. Some benefits are easier for companies to approve than salary increases, so explore creative compensation arrangements.

Build alternative income streams that reduce your dependence on your primary employer and give you leverage in compensation discussions. Consulting work, freelance projects, online businesses, and investment income all contribute to your financial security and negotiating power. The less desperate you are for their money, the more likely they are to pay you what you're worth.

Use competing offers strategically but carefully. Having other options gives you enormous leverage in compensation discussions, but don't make threats you can't follow through on. Get offers in writing before starting negotiations, and be prepared to leave if your current employer won't match market rates.

When companies claim budget constraints, ask what would need to happen for them to find budget for competitive compensation. Would a promotion change the budget category? Would additional responsibilities justify higher pay? Would moving to a different department create opportunities? Make them explain their constraints instead of accepting them as immutable facts.

Address geographic pay adjustments directly if you're being paid less for remote work. Research market rates for your role in major metropolitan areas and make the case that your contributions are worth the same regardless of where you live. Point out that they're getting the same value from your work whether you're in their office or on another continent.

Exercises

Conduct comprehensive market research to establish your true compensation baseline. What are people in similar roles earning at comparable companies? What are the salary ranges for your level of experience and responsibility? What additional compensation could you command with different skills or certifications?

Calculate the real value of your current compensation package by breaking down each component. What's your effective hourly rate including overtime and weekend work? What are your benefits worth in cash terms? What's the realistic value of equity compensation based on current market conditions?

Document your business impact systematically to build a quantitative case for higher compensation. What contributions have you made that created measurable value? What problems have you solved that others couldn't? What would it cost to replace your contributions with external resources?

Develop multiple income streams that reduce your dependence on your primary employer. What skills do you have that others would pay for? What knowledge could you monetize through consulting, teaching, or content creation? What passive income opportunities could you pursue?

Create a compensation negotiation strategy that includes multiple scenarios and fallback positions. What would you accept as a minimal increase? What would represent a win? What non-salary benefits would add value to your package? What would cause you to leave for opportunities elsewhere?

Companies pay what they have to pay, not what you deserve. Your worth is determined by what others are willing to pay for your contributions, not by your needs, your effort, or your loyalty. The market doesn't care about fairness, it cares about value creation and supply and demand.

Compensation negotiations are business discussions, not personal conversations. Don't make it emotional or take rejection personally. Present facts, make reasonable requests, and be prepared to walk away if they won't meet market rates. You're not asking for charity, you're asking to be paid what you're worth.

Your real target isn't your current salary, it's your lifetime earning potential. Sometimes that means leaving for better opportunities. Sometimes it means building skills that command higher compensation. Sometimes it means starting your own business where you control your earning potential.

Get comfortable advocating for yourself financially. Nobody else will do it for you, and nobody should have to. You're responsible for ensuring that you're compensated fairly for the value you create. Don't let false modesty or social conditioning keep you from getting paid what you're worth.

Scripts

Strategy without words is useless in the room. Here are the actual lines for the four situations that derail most compensation conversations.

When they ask your salary expectations before making an offer

The goal is to avoid anchoring low before you know the full scope of the role. Whoever names a number first loses negotiating room.

"I want to make sure we're aligned before I give you a number — can you share the budgeted range for this role? I've done market research on comparable positions and I'd like to see how your range compares before we discuss specifics."

If they push harder and insist on a number first: "Based on my research and experience, I'm targeting the [X to Y] range, with the understanding that total compensation includes [list the key benefits]. Is that in the right territory for this role?" Give a range where your actual target is the bottom of the range.

When they come back with a lowball offer

Don't accept, don't panic, don't apologize. Express enthusiasm for the role while anchoring to the number you actually want.

"I'm genuinely excited about this role and I want to make this work. Based on my research into market rates for this level of experience and responsibility, I was expecting something closer to [your target number]. Is there flexibility to get there?"

Then stop talking. The silence is not yours to fill. Let them respond. First person to speak after the ask usually concedes ground.

When they say "we don't negotiate" or "that's our best offer"

This is a bluff more often than it's a policy. Most companies that claim they don't negotiate have done it last week for someone they wanted badly enough.

"I appreciate you being upfront with me. I want to be equally direct — I've done my research, and the market for this role is running [X to Y]. I'm genuinely interested in joining the team, but I need to be somewhere in that range to make this work. What can we do?"

If they still hold firm, negotiate the non-salary items: signing bonus, remote days, title, earlier performance review, professional development budget, extra PTO. Some of these come from different budget lines and are easier to approve than base salary increases.

When asking for a raise mid-cycle, not at review time

Waiting for the annual review is waiting for the worst possible moment — budgets are already set and increases are already decided. Mid-cycle asks work best right after a visible win, a scope expansion, or when you have a competing offer.

"I wanted to talk to you about my compensation. Since [specific event — the project landed, the scope expanded, the market shifted], I've been doing research and I think there's a gap between what I'm being paid and what this role is worth right now. I'd like to discuss getting to [specific number]. Can we find time to talk through that?"

Come to that meeting with your market data printed out, your accomplishments documented, and a specific number. Not a range — a number. Ranges signal that you'll accept the lower end. Name what you want and let them negotiate down from there, not up from nothing.

Exit Strategy Development

The Problem

Most people stay trapped in jobs they hate because they never develop a realistic plan for leaving. They fantasize about dramatic resignations, dream about starting their own business, or talk endlessly about "someday" making a change, but they never do the work required to make escape possible. They remain psychologically and financially dependent on employers who don't deserve their loyalty or talent.

The exit strategy isn't just about quitting your job, it's about building the financial resources, professional capabilities, and personal resilience that give you genuine freedom of choice. Without a concrete plan, you're always one layoff, one toxic boss, or one corporate restructuring away from desperation. With a solid exit strategy, you can make career decisions from strength instead of fear.

The biggest mistake people make is thinking that exit planning is something you do when you're already miserable. By then, you're operating from desperation instead of strategy, and desperate people make poor decisions. The best time to plan your exit is when you don't need to leave, when you can build your capabilities and resources without the pressure of immediate necessity.

Discussion

I've done this more than once, and the mechanics were the same each time. Once I decided to leave, I had roughly a month before I found a position or a clear next direction. That month had a specific rhythm: take stock of where the finances actually stood, cut back on anything that wasn't essential, and start looking without knowing how long the search would take. That uncertainty is uncomfortable. You can't schedule an exit the way you'd schedule a vacation.

Even after an offer came in, I didn't relax. The fear that it would fall through — that the company would rescind, that the role would evaporate, that something would go wrong at the last moment — stayed with me until I was through the door. An offer is not a job. It's a conditional agreement that both parties can still exit. Treat it that way.

The most important discipline during that period was behavioral. I told nobody. I changed nothing visible — not my effort level, not my attitude, not my interactions with my boss or colleagues. Any shift in behavior signals the decision before you're ready to make it official, and once people sense you're leaving, your situation changes immediately and not in your favor. My boss was always shocked when I gave notice. That shock was the goal. It meant I had protected the process completely.

That sequence — decide, take financial stock, reduce exposure, search in parallel, manage the offer anxiety, maintain the mask, give notice — is a template. It's not glamorous, but it works. The chapter ahead builds out each piece of it in more detail.

Let's start with the financial reality that most people refuse to face. You don't need enough money to retire, but you do need enough money to make choices without desperation driving your decisions. The magic number isn't about luxury, it's about independence. It's the amount that lets you walk away from toxic situations, take calculated risks, and pursue opportunities that don't offer immediate payoffs.

The traditional advice is six months of expenses, but that's survival thinking, not freedom thinking. Six months gives you enough time to panic about finding any job that will pay your bills. Twelve to eighteen months gives you the freedom to be selective about opportunities and the time to transition into something better instead of just different.

Calculate your true monthly expenses, not your current lifestyle costs. What do you need to live on if you eliminated unnecessary spending? Housing, food, utilities, transportation, insurance, debt payments. Strip away the discretionary spending that makes you feel successful but keeps you financially trapped. The lower your true survival number, the more freedom you have.

Skill diversification is your insurance policy against industry disruption and your ticket to better opportunities. The goal isn't to become mediocre at everything, but to develop capabilities that transfer across roles, industries, and economic conditions. Build skills that complement each other and create unique value combinations that are harder to replace or outsource.

Develop these skills without raising suspicion at your current job. Use company time and resources for learning that appears to benefit your current role while building capabilities that serve your long-term goals. Volunteer for cross-functional projects, attend industry conferences, take on assignments that expose you to different aspects of the business.

Network building is about creating relationships that survive job changes and provide opportunities when you need them. Most people only network when they're job searching, which makes them seem desperate and transactional. Real networking happens when you're helping others, sharing knowledge, and building genuine professional relationships.

Focus on building relationships with people outside your current company and industry. Your internal network disappears when you leave, but external relationships can provide opportunities for decades. Invest in relationships with clients, vendors, competitors, and people in adjacent industries who might need your skills.

Side business development while employed is the ultimate exit strategy because it creates alternative income streams and teaches you entrepreneurial skills that make you more valuable as an employee. The goal isn't to replace your day job immediately, but to build something that could eventually provide financial independence.

Start small with skills and knowledge you already have. Consulting, freelancing, online courses, content creation, e-commerce. Test ideas with minimal investment while you still have the safety net of regular employment. Learn about marketing, sales, customer service, and business operations while someone else is paying your bills.

The psychological preparation for career transitions is often more challenging than the financial or professional preparation. Leaving a job, even a job you hate, means leaving familiarity, routine, and identity. You might be miserable, but you know how to be miserable in your current situation. Change requires tolerating uncertainty and discomfort while you figure out new systems and relationships.

Mental health during career transitions requires acknowledging that change is stressful even when it's positive. You might feel anxious, depressed, or confused during the transition period. This doesn't mean you're making a mistake, it means you're human. Build support systems, maintain healthy habits, and get professional help if you need it.

The timing of your exit is almost as important as the preparation. Don't quit during personal crises, family emergencies, or major life changes. Don't leave right before major expenses or during economically uncertain times unless you have no choice. Plan your departure for when you can focus on the transition without other major stressors.

Many people sabotage their exit strategies by talking about them too much or too early. Don't announce your plans to colleagues, don't post about your side business on company social media, and don't give your employer reason to question your commitment before you're ready to leave. Discretion protects your current job while you build alternatives.

Solutions

An effective exit strategy requires systematic planning across multiple areas of your life. Start with an honest assessment of your current situation and a realistic timeline for building the resources you need to create genuine choice in your career.

Calculate your financial runway by tracking your expenses for three months and identifying what you could eliminate in an emergency. Create a separate savings account dedicated to career transition funds and automate contributions to build this fund without thinking about it. This isn't your retirement savings or emergency fund, it's your freedom fund.

Accelerate your savings by increasing income, reducing expenses, or both. Negotiate raises, take on freelance work, sell possessions you don't need, or find ways to reduce fixed costs. Every dollar you save is a day of freedom you're buying for your future self. The faster you build financial independence, the sooner you can make choices based on what you want instead of what you need.

Diversify your skills systematically by identifying capabilities that would make you valuable in multiple industries or roles. Focus on skills that combine technical competence with business understanding. Learn to speak the language of different departments, industries, and business functions so you can translate your expertise to new contexts.

Build your external network through industry events, professional associations, online communities, and informational interviews with people whose careers you admire. Offer value before asking for help. Share knowledge, make introductions, and be genuinely helpful to others. The relationships you build during good times become lifelines during transitions.

Develop multiple income streams that reduce your dependence on any single employer. This might include consulting, teaching, investing, creating digital products, or building businesses around your expertise. The goal is to reach a point where losing your primary job would be inconvenient but not catastrophic.

Document your achievements and build a portfolio of work that demonstrates your capabilities to potential employers or clients. Keep records of problems you've solved, value you've created, and skills you've developed. Create case studies, gather testimonials, and build evidence of your competence that goes beyond your resume.

Prepare mentally for the uncertainty and stress of career transitions by developing coping strategies and support systems. This might include therapy, meditation, exercise, journaling, or other practices that help you manage stress and maintain perspective during difficult periods.

Exercises

Calculate your true financial runway by tracking expenses and identifying your minimum survival budget. How long could you live on your current savings? What would you need to save to have twelve to eighteen months of financial freedom? Create a plan with timelines and milestones for building your freedom fund.

Audit your current skills and identify gaps that limit your career mobility. What capabilities would make you valuable in other industries? What skills could you develop that would increase your income potential? Create a learning plan that builds these capabilities systematically.

Map your professional network and identify relationships that could provide opportunities outside your current company. Who do you know in other industries? What relationships could you build that would expand your options? Develop a networking strategy that focuses on providing value to others.

Research business opportunities that align with your skills and interests. What services could you provide as a consultant or freelancer? What products could you create based on your knowledge? What market needs could you address with your expertise? Start small and test ideas while you're still employed.

Create a transition timeline that balances your need for security with your desire for change. When would be the optimal time to leave your current role? What milestones need to be achieved before you can make the transition safely? What contingency plans do you need if circumstances change?

Exit strategies aren't just about leaving jobs. They're about creating the freedom to make choices based on your goals instead of your fears. The point isn't to become unemployed. It's to build enough options that no single employer controls your destiny.

The best exit strategy is one you never have to use because the process of building it makes you more valuable, more confident, and more capable of creating opportunities wherever you are. But having the option to leave gives you the power to stay on your own terms instead of theirs.

Start building your exit strategy now, while you don't need it. Your future self will thank you for the freedom you're creating today.

Playing the Corporate Game - Strategic Excellence

"If you know the enemy and know yourself, you need not fear the result of a hundred battles." - Sun Tzu

The Problem

Corporate environments reward people who understand the unwritten rules, not necessarily the people who do the best work. You can be brilliant at your job and still get passed over for promotions, excluded from important projects, and eventually pushed out if you don't know how to navigate the political landscape. The game exists whether you choose to play it or not, and refusing to participate is just another way of losing.

The most frustrating part is that the skills that make you good at your job are often different from the skills that make you successful in corporate politics. Technical competence, ethical behavior, and hard work are baseline expectations, not competitive advantages. Success requires understanding how decisions really get made, who has influence, and how to position yourself strategically within systems designed to benefit insiders.

The corporate game isn't fair, logical, or merit-based, but it's predictable once you understand the rules. Companies are hierarchical organizations run by humans with egos, insecurities, and personal agendas. Learning to work within these systems doesn't make you corrupt or unprincipled, it makes you effective at creating the conditions you need to do meaningful work and advance your career.

Discussion

Let's start with visibility management, the art of being seen when it benefits you and invisible when it doesn't. Most people get this backwards. They hide when they should be promoting their achievements and speak up when they should keep quiet. Strategic visibility means understanding when your contributions need to be noticed and when drawing attention could backfire.

Shine during budget planning seasons, performance review periods, and project launches when decision makers are paying attention and looking for people to reward or promote. Make sure your wins are visible to people who matter, not just your immediate team. Volunteer to present results to senior leadership. Send update emails that highlight your contributions to stakeholders who control resources and opportunities.

Hide when there's blame to be assigned, when layoffs are being planned, and when controversial decisions are being made. Don't volunteer for impossible projects that are designed to fail. Avoid being associated with initiatives that leadership doesn't really support. Stay out of interpersonal conflicts that don't directly affect your work or reputation.

Performance reviews are theater designed to justify predetermined decisions while maintaining the illusion of fairness. The actual evaluation happens throughout the year based on your visibility, relationships, and political positioning. The formal review process just documents decisions that have already been made.

Goal setting in performance reviews is a negotiation, not a mandate. Push back on unrealistic expectations while proposing alternatives that demonstrate your strategic thinking. Document everything in writing so there's a record of what was agreed upon. Build in success metrics that you can control rather than outcomes that depend on factors outside your influence.

Meeting survival requires understanding that most meetings aren't about making decisions, they're about information sharing, relationship building, and political positioning. Your job isn't to solve every problem discussed or contribute to every topic. Your job is to appear engaged while identifying information that affects your work and building relationships that serve your interests.

Speak strategically in meetings by asking good questions rather than providing answers to problems you don't own. Volunteer for visible projects that align with your career goals. Support ideas proposed by influential people while distancing yourself from proposals that seem doomed to fail. Take notes so you appear engaged even when the discussion is irrelevant to your work.

Email communication in corporate environments requires understanding that everything you write could be forwarded, saved, and used against you later. Write emails that sound professional when read by your boss's boss. Avoid emotional language, sarcasm, or anything that could be misinterpreted. Use email to create helpful documentation while protecting yourself from future blame.

Managing up is about making your boss successful while building your own reputation and capabilities. This doesn't mean being subservient or sacrificing your principles. It means understanding your manager's pressures and priorities so you can support their goals while advancing your own agenda. The better your boss looks, the more opportunities they can create for you.

Anticipate your manager's needs and solve problems before they become crises. Provide solutions along with problems. Keep them informed about potential issues without creating unnecessary anxiety. Give them credit for successes while taking responsibility for your contributions. Make their job easier while building evidence of your competence and judgment.

The key to playing the corporate game successfully is understanding that it's about relationships and perceptions, not just performance. People make decisions based on limited information, personal biases, and emotional reactions. Your job is to influence those perceptions strategically while maintaining your integrity and building genuine value.

Corporate politics isn't about manipulation or deception, it's about understanding human nature and organizational dynamics. People prefer to work with others they like and trust. They reward loyalty, reliability, and competence in that order. They promote people who make them look good and avoid people who create problems or embarrassment.

Solutions

Playing the corporate game effectively requires developing political intelligence while maintaining your professional standards and personal values. The goal isn't to become a manipulative politician, it's to understand how organizations really work so you can navigate them successfully.

Build relationships strategically by identifying the people who influence decisions that affect your career. This includes your manager's manager, colleagues in other departments, and people who have access to senior leadership. Invest time in these relationships during non-crisis periods so you have allies when you need them.

Create value for influential people by solving problems they care about, even if those problems aren't directly related to your job responsibilities. Volunteer for cross-functional projects that give you exposure to different parts of the organization. Offer to help with initiatives that matter to senior leadership.

Document your contributions systematically so you can articulate your value during performance discussions and promotion opportunities. Keep records of problems you've solved, goals you've achieved, and positive feedback you've received. Use this documentation to build compelling narratives about your impact and potential.

Communicate strategically by tailoring your message to your audience's interests and priorities. When talking to your manager, focus on how your work supports their goals. When presenting to executives, emphasize business impact and strategic alignment. When working with peers, emphasize collaboration and mutual benefit.

Manage your reputation proactively by being reliable, competent, and easy to work with. Deliver what you promise when you promise it. Respond to requests promptly and professionally. Take responsibility for mistakes while highlighting lessons learned. Build a reputation as someone who solves problems rather than creates them.

Navigate office politics by staying neutral in conflicts that don't affect you directly while building alliances with people who share your professional interests. Don't gossip, don't take sides in personality conflicts, and don't get drawn into drama that doesn't serve your career goals.

Time your career moves strategically by understanding organizational cycles and leadership changes. Apply for promotions when budgets are being set, not when they're being cut. Build relationships with rising leaders before they reach positions of power. Position yourself for opportunities that align with company priorities and strategic directions.

Exercises

Map the informal power structure in your organization by identifying who really influences decisions about resources, personnel, and strategic direction. Who has access to senior leadership? Who gets consulted before major decisions? Who are the opinion leaders that others follow? Focus your relationship-building efforts on these influential people.

Audit your current visibility and reputation by getting honest feedback from trusted colleagues about how you're perceived. Are you seen as competent and reliable? Do people know about your contributions? Are you associated with successful projects and positive outcomes? Identify gaps between your performance and your reputation.

Develop a strategic communication plan that ensures your achievements are visible to decision makers. How will you share information about your successes? Who needs to know about your contributions? What forums exist for showcasing your capabilities? Create systematic ways to build awareness of your value.

Practice managing up by understanding your manager's goals, pressures, and priorities. What does success look like from their perspective? What problems keep them awake at night? How can you help them achieve their objectives while advancing your own career? Align your efforts with their needs.

Create a political strategy that positions you for advancement while maintaining your integrity. What relationships do you need to build? What projects should you volunteer for? What skills should you develop? What reputation do you want to build? Make deliberate choices about how you engage with organizational dynamics.

The corporate game exists whether you acknowledge it or not. Choosing not to play doesn't exempt you from the consequences of other people playing. You're not trying to become a scheming politician. You're trying to understand how organizations actually work.

Success in corporate environments requires both competence and political intelligence. You need to be good at your job and good at positioning yourself for opportunities. Neither skill alone is sufficient for long-term career success.

The most successful people are those who understand that corporate environments are human systems with human dynamics. They build genuine relationships, create real value, and position themselves strategically for advancement. They play the game while remaining authentic to their values and goals.

Play smart, not dirty. Win through competence and strategic thinking, not manipulation and deception. The goal is to succeed within corporate systems while building the skills and relationships that give you options beyond any single organization.

Alternative Career Paths - Escape Routes That Work

"The entrepreneur always searches for change, responds to it, and exploits it as an opportunity." - Peter Drucker

The Problem

Traditional employment has become so toxic and unstable that millions of people are looking for alternatives, but most have no realistic plan for transitioning to independent work. They romanticize entrepreneurship without understanding the skills, resources, and mindset required to succeed outside of corporate structures. They dream about freelancing freedom while ignoring the harsh realities of irregular income, self-employment taxes, and the constant hustle for new clients.

The alternative career path mythology sells the fantasy that escaping corporate life automatically leads to fulfillment and financial success. Instagram entrepreneurs and lifestyle bloggers make independent work look easy and glamorous while hiding the failures, stress, and financial instability that most people experience when they first strike out on their own. The reality is that most alternative career paths require more work, not less, especially in the beginning.

The biggest mistake people make is thinking they can jump directly from employee to successful entrepreneur without developing the skills, relationships, and financial resources that independent work requires. They quit their jobs to "follow their passion" without understanding market demand, business fundamentals, or their own capabilities. Most fail within the first year because they confuse having a skill with knowing how to build a business around that skill.

Discussion

Let's start with freelancing, which sounds like the easiest transition but is often the most challenging because it requires you to become a business owner overnight. You're no longer just responsible for doing the work, you're responsible for finding clients, managing projects, handling finances, dealing with contracts, and marketing your services. Most people who try freelancing fail because they focus on the work while ignoring the business side.

Freelancing transition requires building your client base while you're still employed, not after you quit your job. Start taking on small projects in the evenings and weekends to test market demand and develop your business processes. Learn about pricing, contracts, invoicing, and client management before you depend on freelance income to pay your bills. The goal is to replace your salary with client revenue before you give up the security of employment.

The feast-or-famine cycle destroys most freelancers because they don't understand how to build sustainable client relationships. They complete projects and then scramble to find new work instead of developing ongoing relationships that provide steady income. Successful freelancers focus on building long-term partnerships with clients who need their services repeatedly instead of constantly hunting for one-off projects.

Consulting is freelancing for people with expertise that commands premium pricing, but it requires different skills and positioning. Consultants solve strategic problems instead of completing tactical tasks. They're hired for their judgment and experience, not their ability to execute projects. The transition from employee to consultant requires reframing your experience as valuable expertise that organizations will pay premium rates to access.

Consulting business development starts with identifying problems you can solve that are worth more to clients than they cost to fix. You need to understand the business impact of the problems you solve and position yourself as someone who can deliver measurable results. This requires developing business acumen, not just technical skills. You need to speak the language of executives and understand how your work contributes to organizational success.

The hardest part about consulting is pricing your services based on value instead of time. Employees think in terms of hourly wages, but consultants need to think in terms of outcomes and impact. A strategy that saves a company millions of dollars is worth hundreds of thousands to develop, regardless of how many hours it takes. Learning to price based on value instead of effort is essential for consulting success.

Small business development is the path for people who want to build something scalable instead of trading time for money indefinitely. But most people who start small businesses fail because they don't understand the difference between being self-employed and owning a business. Self-employment means you own a job. Business ownership means you own a system that generates value without your constant involvement.

Small businesses succeed when they solve real problems for customers better than existing alternatives. The key is starting with market demand instead of personal passion. Find a group of people who have a problem they're willing to pay to solve, then build a business around addressing that problem. Passion for the problem domain helps, but passion for the solution is more important than passion for the work itself.

The biggest small business mistake is trying to do everything yourself instead of building systems and hiring people who can execute those systems. Successful business owners focus on strategy, relationships, and growth while delegating operational tasks to others. This requires learning to manage people, processes, and finances instead of just being good at the core service or product.

Passive income development is the holy grail that most people never achieve because they misunderstand what "passive" means. Truly passive income requires upfront investment of time, money, or both to create assets that generate revenue without ongoing effort. Real estate investments, dividend-paying stocks, royalties from creative work, or automated businesses can provide passive income, but building these income streams requires active effort initially.

The passive income mythology ignores the fact that most income streams require ongoing maintenance, optimization, and reinvestment to remain viable. Rental properties need management and maintenance. Investment portfolios need monitoring and rebalancing. Digital products need updates and marketing. The goal isn't to eliminate all work, it's to decouple your income from your time so you can earn money while focusing on other priorities.

Geographic arbitrage and location independence have become more viable with remote work technology, but they require planning and careful execution. The idea is to earn income in high-wage markets while living in low-cost locations, maximizing your purchasing power and lifestyle quality. This works best for people with skills that can be delivered digitally and clients who care about outcomes instead of location.

Location independence requires more than just the ability to work remotely. You need to understand international tax implications, healthcare options, visa requirements, and cultural considerations. You need reliable internet, appropriate time zone overlap with clients, and the personal flexibility to adapt to different environments. The digital nomad lifestyle looks glamorous on social media but requires planning and adaptation skills.

Solutions

Successful alternative career paths require systematic planning, skill development, and gradual transition instead of dramatic career changes. The goal is to build new income streams while maintaining financial stability, not to jump into entrepreneurship without preparation.

Start your transition while still employed by testing your ideas and building capabilities with minimal risk. Use evenings and weekends to develop freelance clients, create digital products, or explore business opportunities. Treat these activities as market research and skill development instead of immediate income replacement. Learn what works and what doesn't while you still have a steady paycheck.

Develop the business skills that employees rarely need but entrepreneurs can't survive without. Learn about marketing, sales, finance, operations, and customer service. Understand how to price services, manage cash flow, handle contracts, and build sustainable client relationships. These skills are more important than technical expertise for independent work success.

Build your professional network outside your current company and industry. Independent workers succeed through relationships and referrals more than marketing and advertising. Invest in relationships with potential clients, partners, and collaborators who can provide opportunities and support. The stronger your network, the easier it becomes to find clients and grow your business.

Create multiple income streams instead of depending on a single source of revenue. Combine freelance work, consulting projects, digital products, and passive income investments to build a diversified portfolio that can withstand economic changes and market fluctuations. Multiple income streams provide security that single employers can't offer.

Exercises

Research alternative career opportunities that align with your skills, interests, and market demand. What services could you provide as a freelancer? What expertise could you package as a consulting offering? What business opportunities exist in your field? What passive income streams could you develop? Start with realistic assessment of your capabilities and market conditions.

Test your alternative career ideas with minimal investment while still employed. Take on small freelance projects, create sample consulting proposals, develop prototype products, or explore business partnerships. Use these experiments to validate demand and refine your approach before committing time or money.

Develop the business skills you'll need for independent work by taking courses, reading books, or working with mentors who have succeeded in alternative career paths. Focus on marketing, sales, finance, and operations instead of just technical skills. Learn from people who have built successful independent careers instead of those who just talk about entrepreneurship.

Build your financial runway to support the transition to independent work. Calculate how much money you need to cover expenses during the startup phase. Create separate savings for business investment and personal survival. Understand the tax implications and financial requirements of different alternative career paths.

Create a transition timeline that balances security with progress toward independence. When will you start building alternative income streams? What milestones need to be achieved before you can reduce dependence on traditional employment? How will you measure success and adjust your strategy based on results?

Alternative career paths aren't easier than traditional employment, they're different. Different skills, different mindsets, different approaches to risk and reward. The people who succeed in independent work are those who understand the differences and prepare for them.

You're not trying to escape work, you're trying to gain control over it. Independent career paths give you more autonomy and potentially higher earning potential, but they also require more responsibility and risk tolerance. Make sure you're moving toward something you want instead of just away from something you hate.

Alternative careers work best for people who are self-motivated, comfortable with uncertainty, and willing to learn business skills beyond their core expertise. If these descriptions fit you, independent work might provide the freedom and fulfillment that traditional employment can't offer. If not, focus on finding better employers instead of eliminating employers entirely.

I can speak to this from experience. I left a twenty-year career at Trader Joe's at 53, where I'd spent the last stretch as Director of Computer Operations. I left on good terms and with genuine respect for the company. But I had 33 years of experience and no degree, and the degree blocked the CIO path I wanted. So I went looking externally — CIO roles, director roles. Nobody would take me. Nobody said it was age. Nobody had to. The pattern was clear enough.

So I stopped interviewing and started building. Within a year I had sold $35,000 worth of product on eBay, generated $10,000 in affiliate marketing income, earned $25,000 from book sales, and brought in $50,000 in ghostwriting fees. That's $120,000 in the first year from four income streams that didn't exist when I started.

None of it was handed to me and none of it was easy. But none of it required a hiring manager to say yes, either. The corporate market had decided I wasn't worth the risk. Turns out the feeling was mutual.

Psychological Warfare Defense - Protecting Your Mind

"It is no measure of health to be well adjusted to a profoundly sick society." - Jiddu Krishnamurti

---

The Problem

Modern workplaces systematically damage mental health while gaslighting employees into believing their psychological distress is a personal failure instead of a predictable response to toxic environments. Companies create conditions that would break most people and then offer wellness programs and mental health resources as if meditation apps can fix what systemic exploitation created.

The corporate wellness industrial complex is designed to shift responsibility for workplace psychological damage from organizations to people. Instead of addressing the root causes of stress, burnout, and depression (unrealistic expectations, toxic management, job insecurity, and work-life imbalance), they teach you breathing exercises and mindfulness techniques. It's like offering bandages to someone they're stabbing.

What makes it harder to fight is how normalized workplace psychological abuse has become. People accept anxiety, depression, and burnout as inevitable parts of having a career instead of recognizing them as symptoms of dysfunctional systems. They blame themselves for not being resilient enough instead of questioning why their work environment requires superhuman resilience just to survive.

Discussion

Let's start with burnout, which isn't just being tired or stressed from work. Burnout is a psychological condition characterized by emotional exhaustion, depersonalization, and a reduced sense of personal accomplishment. It's what happens when you're exposed to chronic workplace stress without adequate resources or support to cope. Your nervous system gets stuck in survival mode, and your capacity for normal human functioning deteriorates.

Burnout recognition requires understanding that it's not a character flaw or a sign of weakness. It's a predictable response to unsustainable working conditions. You might feel emotionally numb toward your work, cynical about your organization, physically exhausted despite getting adequate sleep, or unable to concentrate on tasks that used to be easy. Your immune system might be compromised, leading to frequent illness.

The corporate response to burnout is usually more of what caused it in the first place. They'll suggest better time management, stress reduction techniques, or taking vacation time to "recharge." But burnout isn't caused by poor personal habits, it's caused by systemic problems that vacation time can't fix. Coming back from vacation to the same toxic environment just restarts the burnout cycle.

Anxiety in high-stress work environments is often dismissed as normal job pressure, but chronic workplace anxiety can develop into serious mental health conditions that affect every area of your life. Your nervous system can't distinguish between real threats and workplace stressors, so constant deadlines, difficult bosses, and job insecurity trigger the same biological responses as physical danger.

Workplace anxiety manifests as physical symptoms: racing heart, difficulty breathing, muscle tension, headaches, digestive problems, and sleep disturbances. You might feel constantly on edge, have trouble concentrating, or experience panic attacks during or in anticipation of work situations. These aren't signs that you're not cut out for your job, they're signs that your job is not compatible with human psychological health.

The anxiety-productivity trap convinces people that stress and anxiety are necessary for high performance. Some companies deliberately create high-anxiety environments because they believe fear motivates people to work harder. But chronic anxiety impairs cognitive function, decision-making ability, and creative thinking. The performance improvement from short-term stress doesn't justify the long-term psychological damage.

Depression in workplace contexts often gets misdiagnosed as burnout or stress because the symptoms can overlap. But depression involves persistent feelings of hopelessness, worthlessness, and loss of interest in activities that used to bring pleasure. When your job systematically undermines your sense of competence, autonomy, and purpose, depression becomes a rational response to irrational circumstances.

Situational despair is different from clinical depression, though they can look similar from the outside. If your psychological distress is directly related to work circumstances and improves when you're away from work, you might be dealing with situational despair caused by your environment instead of clinical depression requiring medical treatment. Both deserve attention, but they require different approaches.

The "tough it out" mentality prevents people from getting help when they need it most. There's a pervasive belief that seeking therapy or taking medication for work-related mental health issues is a sign of weakness or professional inadequacy. This stigma keeps people suffering in silence while their psychological health deteriorates to the point where it affects their ability to work and function in other areas of life.

Therapy selection for work-related mental health issues requires finding someone who understands workplace dynamics and doesn't just focus on helping you adapt to toxic situations. Some therapists will try to help you become more resilient to abuse instead of recognizing that the problem is the abuse itself. You need someone who can help you distinguish between problems you need to solve and problems you need to escape.

Corporate Employee Assistance Programs (EAPs) are often inadequate for serious mental health issues because they're designed to provide minimal intervention instead of comprehensive care. They might offer a few free sessions with therapists who have no ongoing relationship with you and limited ability to provide continuous care. EAPs are better than nothing, but they're not substitutes for real mental health treatment.

Stress management techniques taught in corporate wellness programs often focus on helping you tolerate more stress instead of addressing the sources of stress. Mindfulness meditation, breathing exercises, and yoga can be helpful tools, but they're not solutions to systemic workplace problems. Learning to relax doesn't help if you're still dealing with impossible deadlines, toxic management, or job insecurity.

Solutions

Protecting your mental health in toxic work environments requires recognizing that your psychological distress is a rational response to irrational circumstances, not a personal failure that requires you to become more resilient. Maintain your mental health while building alternatives. You're not trying to become invulnerable to workplace abuse — you're trying to limit your exposure to it.

Start by acknowledging that your work environment might be damaging your mental health. This isn't weakness or failure, it's pattern recognition. If you feel consistently anxious, depressed, or exhausted in ways that seem disproportionate to normal work stress, trust your instincts. Your nervous system is giving you important information about your environment.

Establish boundaries that protect your mental health even if they conflict with workplace expectations. This might mean not checking email after hours, taking lunch breaks, using vacation time without feeling guilty, or refusing to work excessive overtime except in genuine emergencies. Your mental health is more important than appearing dedicated to people who don't care about your wellbeing.

Build support systems outside of work that can provide perspective and validation. Work environments can distort your sense of reality, making toxic behavior seem normal and reasonable responses seem extreme. Friends, family members, or support groups outside your workplace can help you maintain perspective on what's reasonable to expect from employment.

Seek professional help when workplace stress starts affecting your ability to function in other areas of your life. If you're having trouble sleeping, maintaining relationships, enjoying activities you used to love, or managing basic life tasks, you might need more support than self-help techniques can provide. There's no shame in getting professional help for problems caused by your work environment.

When selecting a therapist, look for someone who understands workplace dynamics and won't just focus on helping you adapt to toxic situations. Ask potential therapists about their experience with work-related stress, burnout, and workplace trauma. You want someone who can help you distinguish between reasonable workplace challenges and unreasonable working conditions.

Develop stress management practices that don't depend on your employer's wellness programs. Regular exercise, adequate sleep, healthy eating, social connections, and activities that bring you joy are more important for mental health than any corporate mindfulness program. Build habits that support your psychological wellbeing independent of workplace initiatives.

Create mental separation between work and personal life through rituals that help your nervous system transition between work mode and personal mode. This might include changing clothes when you get home, taking a walk after work, or having a routine that signals the end of the workday. Without clear boundaries, work stress bleeds into every area of your life.

Assess your current mental health honestly by tracking your mood, energy levels, and stress responses for two weeks. How do you feel on Sunday nights? How do you feel Monday mornings? How does your mood change throughout the workweek? Look for patterns that might indicate workplace-related mental health issues.

Identify workplace stressors that affect your mental health. Is it your manager, your workload, your colleagues, the company culture, or the nature of the work itself? Understanding what's causing your distress helps you develop targeted strategies for protecting yourself or planning your escape.

Build a mental health support network that includes professional resources, personal relationships, and self-care practices. Who can you talk to when work stress becomes overwhelming? What professional resources are available to you? What activities help you manage stress and maintain perspective?

Develop stress management practices that work for your lifestyle and preferences. This might include exercise, meditation, creative activities, social connection, or time in nature. Experiment with different approaches to find what helps you maintain mental health during stressful periods.

Create a mental health action plan for when workplace stress becomes unmanageable. What are the warning signs that you need additional support? Who will you contact for help? What steps will you take to protect your mental health if your work environment becomes unbearable?

Your mental health is more important than any job. No amount of money or career advancement is worth destroying your psychological wellbeing. Jobs are replaceable. Your mental health is not.

If your workplace is systematically damaging your mental health, the problem is the workplace, not you. Don't let toxic environments convince you that your reasonable responses to unreasonable treatment are signs of personal inadequacy. Trust your instincts and protect yourself accordingly.

Mental health treatment for work-related issues isn't just about managing symptoms, it's about developing the clarity and confidence you need to make decisions that serve your long-term wellbeing. Sometimes that means finding ways to cope with your current situation. Sometimes it means building an exit strategy. A good therapist can help you figure out which approach serves your interests.

Your psychological health affects every area of your life. Protecting it isn't selfish or weak, it's essential for your ability to build the career and life you want. Don't sacrifice your mental health for employers who wouldn't hesitate to replace you if it served their interests.

Life Design - Building Around Work, Not Through It

The Problem

Most people structure their entire lives around their jobs, as if employment were the foundation upon which everything else rests. They choose where to live based on commute times, when to have children based on maternity leave policies, and how to spend their time based on what their employer demands. This backwards approach makes every other aspect of life dependent on the whims of organizations that could eliminate your position without warning.

The traditional life model (education, career, marriage, house, kids, retirement) was designed for an economy that no longer exists. It assumed stable long-term employment, predictable career progression, employer-provided benefits, and reliable pension systems. That world is gone, but people keep trying to build their lives according to rules that no longer apply to economic realities.

The most dangerous assumption is that work will provide meaning, identity, and purpose. Companies love employees who derive their self-worth from their job titles and professional achievements because it makes them willing to sacrifice everything else for career advancement. But basing your identity on your employment makes you psychologically vulnerable to every corporate restructuring, layoff, and career setback.

Discussion

Let's start with family and relationship protection, because this is the arena where they do the most damage and get away with it most easily. The trick is that they don't come for your family openly. They do it through guilt, expectation creep, and the slow normalization of availability. Your manager doesn't say "miss your kid's birthday." They say "I know it's short notice, but this is really important." Enough of those and you've accidentally traded the things that matter for a track record of being a team player.

Corporate culture has spent decades making workaholism look like virtue. The person who eats lunch at their desk is "dedicated." The person who takes a real lunch break is "not that serious." The person who leaves at 5:30 is "checked out." They've constructed a moral framework where sacrificing your personal life is evidence of professional worth. It isn't. It's evidence that you've accepted their terms without negotiating.

The challenge is that family-destroying work cultures are often the highest-paying and most prestigious. Companies that demand sixty-hour weeks, constant availability, and frequent travel often offer the best salaries and career advancement opportunities. You have to decide whether the financial benefits are worth the relationship costs, because you can't have both simultaneously. What they won't tell you is that you don't get that time back. The quarter your kid needed you, and you were on a call, is gone. That's not pessimism. That's math.

Relationship protection extends beyond immediate family to friendships and community connections. Work environments that promote competition, secrecy, and fear make it difficult to maintain the trust and vulnerability that real friendships require. You might find yourself too exhausted to invest in friendships or too stressed to be emotionally available to friends who need support.

Here's what they've never told you about financial planning: the advice that gets promoted inside corporate America is the advice that keeps you dependent on corporate America. Max out your 401(k) through payroll deduction. Build equity in a house you can't easily sell. Accumulate lifestyle expenses that require your current salary to maintain. Every piece of that advice, individually reasonable, collectively creates a person who cannot afford to leave a bad situation. That's not an accident. Financial planning for a world where job security doesn't exist requires ignoring most of what HR's financial wellness seminars tell you.

The six-month emergency fund advice was designed for a world where layoffs were rare and job searches took weeks. That world is gone. In an economy where searches take months and transitions can take a year, six months gets you to desperation, not stability. Aim for twelve to eighteen months of liquid savings. Yes, that's a big number. It's also the difference between leaving a toxic situation on your terms and staying because you have no choice.

The standard investment advice — pile everything into tax-advantaged accounts — works great if you never need the money before 59½. In practice, career transitions don't wait for retirement age. If a layoff or a toxic situation forces a move, you need money you can actually reach. Build across account types: some in retirement accounts for the long game, some in taxable accounts for the short game. Flexibility is worth more than marginal tax efficiency when your income is at risk.

Healthcare is the trap that keeps more people in bad jobs than any other single factor. Companies know this. The moment you have a chronic condition, a family member on your plan, or significant out-of-pocket exposure, they own you. You won't leave because you can't afford to lose coverage. They haven't said a word about it, but the calculation is built into how they structure benefits. Breaking that trap requires building a health strategy that doesn't depend on them.

The practical side: stay healthy enough that coverage gaps don't become crises. Exercise and preventive care aren't self-help clichés here, they're financial strategy. Every avoided emergency room visit is leverage you keep. If you're planning a job transition, front-load your preventive care while you still have coverage and before the deductible resets.

If you're in a high-deductible plan, max your HSA every year. It's the one financial account that is triple tax-advantaged — pre-tax contributions, tax-free growth, tax-free withdrawal for medical expenses — and unused balances roll over forever. At 65 it converts to a regular retirement account. Most people leave this money sitting in a low-interest cash account inside the HSA; invest it instead. It's one of the few places the system actually works in your favor, so use it.

Here's the retirement system in plain terms: they eliminated pensions so you bear all the risk. They created 401(k)s as a replacement, then loaded them with high-fee investment options that benefit fund managers more than you. Social Security is perpetually one political cycle away from cuts. They designed the entire system to keep you working as long as possible and feeling behind no matter how much you've saved. Start early, save more than they suggest, and build income outside of employer-controlled accounts.

The 65-year retirement model was built around a life expectancy of 68. You will almost certainly live longer than that, possibly much longer, while the benefits designed for that model keep shrinking. Don't plan for retirement as a finish line. Plan for multiple career phases, income sources, and the very real possibility that the traditional retirement age will be pushed higher by the time you get there. Financial independence — work as optional, not mandatory — is a better target than retirement at a specific age.

The people who actually exit the system early aren't usually the ones who saved harder inside it — they're the ones who stopped needing as much. Lower fixed costs, passive income streams, location-independent work, businesses that run without constant management. Any combination of these reduces how much you need the system to function, which is a different goal than accumulating enough to fund the lifestyle you have now.

They'll try to sell you the idea that your legacy is the product you shipped, the company you built, the brand you served. It costs them nothing and buys enormous loyalty. But legacy that depends on an employer is fragile — companies get acquired, restructured, or deleted. The things that outlast all of it are the relationships you kept, the people you helped, and the work that had nothing to do with your title.

Meaning at work is usually manufactured. Companies invest in mission statements and culture decks because purpose-driven employees work harder for less. The projects that feel important today get cancelled or forgotten. The company that makes you feel like you're changing the world might not exist in five years. Build meaning in places they can't touch.

The things that actually hold up over time — the friendships, the creative work, the people you helped when they needed it, the communities you were part of — none of those come with a title or a quarterly review. They don't disappear when the company restructures. Build more of those. They're not the consolation prize for a career that didn't go the way you planned. They're the point.

Solutions

A life built around work instead of through it requires inverting the traditional priority structure. Work becomes a tool for supporting the life you want to live instead of the foundation that determines how you can live. This shift in perspective changes how you make decisions about careers, money, relationships, and time.

Start by defining what a good life looks like for you independent of career considerations. What relationships matter most? What activities bring you joy and fulfillment? What kind of community do you want to be part of? What legacy do you want to leave? Use these answers to guide career decisions instead of letting career opportunities dictate life choices.

Create non-negotiable boundaries around the things that matter most to you. This might mean refusing jobs that require excessive travel if family time is a priority. It might mean turning down promotions that would require relocating away from community connections. It might mean accepting lower salaries in exchange for better work-life balance.

Build financial independence strategies that don't depend on traditional employment benefits. Maximize tax-advantaged savings accounts, build diversified investment portfolios, and create multiple income streams that reduce dependence on any single employer. The goal is to reach a point where work is optional instead of necessary for survival.

Invest in relationships and activities that provide meaning and identity outside of professional achievement. Develop skills and interests that aren't related to your career. Build friendships based on shared values instead of professional networking. Contribute to causes and communities that matter to you regardless of career benefits.

Design lifestyle choices that prioritize sustainability over optimization. Choose housing, transportation, and consumption patterns that you can maintain during periods of unemployment or career transition. Avoid lifestyle inflation that makes you dependent on high income levels to maintain basic satisfaction.

Exercises

Define your life priorities independent of career considerations. What relationships are most important to you? What activities bring you the most satisfaction? What values guide your decisions? What would a meaningful life look like if career success weren't a factor?

Audit your current life structure to identify areas where work demands are compromising other priorities. How much time and energy does your job consume? What relationships are suffering because of work stress? What activities have you stopped doing because of career demands?

Create a financial independence plan that reduces dependence on employment benefits and traditional retirement models. How much money do you need to feel secure during career transitions? What investment strategies align with your risk tolerance and timeline? What alternative income streams could you develop?

Develop interests and relationships that provide meaning outside of professional achievement. What activities bring you joy that aren't related to your career? What communities could you contribute to? What skills could you develop for personal satisfaction instead of professional advancement?

Design lifestyle choices that prioritize flexibility and sustainability over status and optimization. What changes could you make to reduce your financial dependence on high income? What possessions or commitments could you eliminate to increase your freedom? What would a simpler but more satisfying life look like?

Your job is one part of your life, not the organizing principle around which everything else revolves. Companies want you to believe work should be your primary source of identity and meaning because it makes you easier to control. The most fulfilling lives are built around things that survive any employer.

Life design around work requires courage to prioritize what matters most to you over what society expects or what employers demand. It means making decisions based on your values instead of external pressure. It means building security and meaning through multiple sources instead of depending on employment to provide everything.

The goal isn't to eliminate work from your life or to avoid professional achievement. The goal is to ensure that work serves your life instead of consuming it. When you build a rich, meaningful life outside of work, you become less vulnerable to workplace toxicity and more capable of making career decisions from strength instead of desperation.

Your life is more important than your career. Make sure you're building it that way.

Future-Proofing Your Career - Adaptation Strategies

"It is not the strongest of the species that survives, nor the most intelligent, but the one most responsive to change." - Charles Darwin

The Problem

The pace of change in modern careers has accelerated beyond most people's ability to adapt. Industries that seemed stable for decades disappear within years. Skills that took years to master become obsolete overnight. Companies that dominated markets vanish while startups become global powers faster than traditional organizations can respond to emails. Most people are still planning their careers as if the economy were predictable and stable when the only constant is disruption.

The traditional career advice of "find your passion and stick with it" has become dangerous in an economy where entire industries can be automated, regulated out of existence, or disrupted by technologies that didn't exist five years ago. Following your passion might lead you down a career path that dead-ends just as you reach your peak earning years, leaving you overspecialized in skills nobody needs anymore.

The worst part is that the people giving career advice (university professors, career counselors, HR professionals, and management consultants) are often the least equipped to understand how rapidly the economy is changing. They're advising you based on career models that worked in their past instead of economic realities that will shape your future. They're preparing you for the last war while the next one has already started.

Discussion

Let's start with industry trend analysis, which most people ignore until it's too late to matter. By the time mass media is discussing how artificial intelligence is changing your field, early adopters have already gained years of advantage while late adapters are scrambling to catch up. Learning to identify and respond to industry trends before they become obvious separates career winners from career casualties.

Industry trend analysis requires looking beyond your immediate job responsibilities to understand what's coming before your employer decides to tell you about it — which, based on recent history, they won't do until the day you're handed a box. Companies have known for years which roles AI would affect. They didn't warn anyone. They kept collecting labor at existing prices until the cost savings made a mass restructuring worth the bad press. By the time the news cycle covers "AI eliminating X jobs," hundreds of thousands of people in X are already behind. You're trying to see that coming earlier than they want you to.

The challenge is cutting through the corporate noise. Your company will announce every technology trend that makes them look forward-thinking and bury every one that signals your job is at risk. They'll roll out AI tools with great fanfare and frame it as "augmenting" your work, right up until the quarter when augmented turns into replaced. Don't wait for them to tell you your role is in danger. That conversation happens in the boardroom months before it happens to you.

Most people wait until trends are affecting their daily work before they adapt, which is exactly how companies prefer it. Reactive employees are cheaper to manage. They're too busy catching up to negotiate from strength. The time to build new skills is when you don't desperately need them yet, when you still have the leverage of being currently employed and the bandwidth to learn without panic.

Technology adoption without becoming obsolete requires finding the balance between being an early adopter and avoiding every shiny new tool that promises to revolutionize productivity. The goal isn't to use every new technology, it's to understand which technologies will enhance your capabilities and which will replace your job entirely.

Technology should extend what you can do, not replace what you do. Focus on tools that make you faster, sharper, or more capable in areas where human judgment matters. If a technology can fully automate your work, learn to operate that technology — become the person who runs it, not the person it replaces.

They're counting on you to frame this as a technical challenge rather than a financial one. If you're thinking "how do I stay current with AI tools," you're asking their question. The better question is "which of my skills can they not automate, and how do I make sure I'm paid accordingly for the ones they can't." That reframe changes everything about how you invest your time.

AI and automation will continue eliminating routine tasks while creating opportunities for people who can work effectively with these technologies. The winners will be those who learn to use AI for research, analysis, content creation, and problem-solving while focusing their human attention on judgment, creativity, relationship-building, and strategic thinking.

Stay informed about technological developments in your field without getting overwhelmed by the pace of change. Follow thought leaders who understand both technology and business applications. Experiment with new tools in low-risk situations. Learn enough about emerging technologies to have informed conversations with specialists without trying to become an expert in everything.

Here's what companies know about your professional network that they're counting on you not to notice: an internal-only network disappears the moment you leave. All those relationships you built over years — your manager's trust, the goodwill with cross-functional teams, the institutional knowledge of who actually makes things happen — none of it transfers. It's locked behind a badge that gets deactivated the day you're out. That's not an accident. Companies benefit enormously when your most valuable professional relationships are contained within their walls. It gives them leverage and limits your options.

Your network needs to evolve continuously and it needs to exist primarily outside your current employer. The relationships that matter for your future aren't your colleagues — they're the people in your industry, your field, and adjacent domains who will still know you after the next restructuring. Build relationships with people ahead of where you want to go, alongside where you are now, and behind where you've been. The network you want is one your employer can't delete.

Professional relationships require ongoing maintenance rather than periodic activation when you need something. The people who can actually help you — who will take your call, vouch for you, or think of you when something opens up — are the ones who've seen you consistently, not just when you were job hunting. Invest in these relationships when you don't need anything. That's when it counts.

Remote work has made this harder and more important at the same time. You can now build relationships with people anywhere, but casual proximity no longer does the work for you. You have to be deliberate about it. The people who maintained external networks through the remote work transition are dramatically better positioned than those who let geography become an excuse for professional isolation.

Most technical skills have expiration dates. That's not a neutral observation about technology — it's a structural feature that benefits employers. When your skills are constantly expiring, you're perpetually catching up on your own time and your own money, while the company harvests the capability once you've paid for it. The solution isn't to learn faster. It's to develop learning agility — the ability to acquire new capabilities quickly when demand emerges — so you stop being trapped by the hamster wheel.

The half-life of technical skills will keep shrinking. Programming languages, platforms, and methodologies that seem current today will be legacy in five years. Don't try to predict which skills will hold their value. Instead, get very good at learning new things efficiently. The person who can get to competence in six weeks is more valuable than the person who spent two years becoming an expert in last year's stack.

The entire point of this chapter is to stop being on their timeline. They benefit from reactive employees — workers who are always catching up, always dependent on the next employer to define what skills matter, always building networks inside the company walls they're currently trapped behind. Future-proofing isn't about predicting the future. It's about making yourself harder to trap. Build the network they can't take. Develop the learning speed they can't automate. Stay far enough ahead that when the next restructuring announcement drops, you're already somewhere else in your head — even if you're still at your desk.

Your Career in the Age of Corporate Brutality

"The most powerful weapon against the corporate machine is an employee who truly understands their own value and refuses to accept less." - Richard G. Lowe

Where You Started

Remember when you picked up this book? You were probably afraid of losing your job, grateful for whatever scraps they threw you, believing their narratives about loyalty and hard work paying off. You might have been dealing with a toxic boss, feeling trapped by golden handcuffs, or wondering why you felt so miserable despite having what everyone told you was a "good job."

You were operating from their playbook, following their rules, accepting their definition of success. You thought the problem was you: not resilient enough, not skilled enough, not dedicated enough. You blamed yourself for reasonable reactions to unreasonable treatment. You felt guilty for wanting more than they were willing to give.

Where You Are Now

You're in complete control of your career trajectory. You understand the game, you have the tools, and you know your worth. You're no longer afraid of them because you've built something they can't take away: your own security system.

You see through their manipulation tactics. When they talk about "culture fit," you hear "compliance requirement." When they offer "competitive compensation," you research actual market rates. When they promise "career development," you build your own skills and network. When they demand loyalty, you give professionalism in return.

You've learned to protect your mental health, document everything, build multiple income streams, and maintain relationships that survive job changes. You know how to negotiate from strength, manage up without losing your dignity, and recognize toxic environments before they damage you.

Most importantly, you've discovered that your value isn't determined by their recognition, your security isn't dependent on their approval, and your future isn't limited by their vision. You've built a career that serves your life instead of consuming it.

Your Victory Conditions

Success is no longer defined by climbing their ladder or earning their approval. Victory is having options. Victory is sleeping peacefully because you've built multiple income streams, marketable skills, and exit strategies. Victory is negotiating from strength because you're prepared to walk away.

Victory looks like turning down opportunities that don't serve your goals, even when other people think you're crazy. It looks like setting boundaries that protect your time and energy, even when it disappoints people who expect unlimited access. It looks like making career decisions based on your values instead of their expectations.

Victory is the freedom to take calculated risks because you've built the financial and psychological resources to handle uncertainty. It's the confidence to start your own business, change industries, or relocate for better opportunities because you're not trapped by fear and financial desperation.

But the biggest victory is peace of mind. You no longer lie awake at night worrying about layoffs, performance reviews, or toxic colleagues because you've built defenses against all of these threats. You sleep well because you know you can handle whatever corporate dysfunction they throw at you.

Your New Operating System

Every decision you make now comes from confidence, not fear. Every conversation with management comes from leverage, not desperation. Every career move comes from strategic thinking, not reactive panic.

You approach job interviews as mutual evaluation sessions where you're assessing whether they deserve your talent, not just hoping they'll accept your application. You negotiate compensation based on market value, not gratitude for whatever they offer. You build relationships based on mutual benefit, not one-sided loyalty.

When toxic situations arise, you respond strategically instead of emotionally. You document problems, build alliances, and execute solutions that protect your interests. You know when to fight, when to adapt, and when to leave. You're playing chess while they're still playing checkers.

Your new operating system runs on abundance thinking instead of scarcity mindset. You see opportunities everywhere because you're not desperately clinging to any single option. You take intelligent risks because you've built the resources to handle setbacks. You invest in relationships because you understand that success is a team sport.

Your Next Move

The game never ends, it just gets easier. Keep adapting, keep building, keep growing your options. Industries will change, technologies will evolve, and economic conditions will shift. You now understand what's actually happening and what to do about it.

Keep developing your capabilities, expanding your network, and building income streams that don't depend on any one company's goodwill. Stay informed about what's coming in your industry without getting paralyzed by it. Start building the relationships and habits this book describes.

The Final Truth

You are now dangerous to their exploitation model, and that's exactly where you want to be. You understand their tactics, you've built defenses against their manipulation, and you've created alternatives to their systems. You're no longer dependent on their approval or afraid of their threats.

You've learned to play the game better than the people who created it. Use that power wisely.

Your career belongs to you now. Make it count.

About the Author

Richard Lowe, known professionally as "The Writing King," brings an extraordinary blend of technical expertise, business leadership, and creative excellence to professional ghostwriting. With 45+ years of documented experience spanning major retail and technology leadership, emergency response certification, and creative industries, Richard has established himself as a premier ghostwriter who "speaks fluent nerd"—a unique positioning that lets him serve clients traditional specialists can't reach.

Professional Foundation & Leadership Experience

Richard's career began during computing's most demanding era, managing PDP-11 systems and hand-coding assembly language when starting a computer meant toggling physical switches in correct binary sequences. This technical foundation evolved into executive leadership roles, including 20 years as Director of Computer Operations at Trader Joe's, where he managed IT infrastructure supporting $16 billion in operations across 474+ stores. He led two major digital transformations, oversaw eight distribution centers, and maintained perfect PCI compliance records throughout his tenure.

His technology leadership extends to specialized SCADA systems for major water utilities, pioneering fraud detection algorithms that established foundations for modern AI-driven security systems, and disaster recovery planning for critical infrastructure. This deep technical background enables him to work effectively with biotech CEOs requiring API knowledge, tech executives needing complex concept translation, and industry leaders demanding both technical accuracy and compelling narrative.

Publishing Portfolio & Client Success

With 113+ books published (63 self-published titles and 50+ professional ghostwriting projects), Richard has achieved remarkable commercial success and client outcomes. His "Focus on LinkedIn" became a bestseller with 15,000 copies sold in three days, reaching #43 in all Kindle rankings and receiving professional translations into seven languages.

Most significantly, Richard's ghostwriting has generated transformational business results for clients. One European Fortune 50 manager leveraged his ghostwritten book to secure $30 million in venture capital and completely transform his career from overlooked manager to recognized industry leader earning premium speaking fees. Multiple clients have achieved TEDx speaking opportunities, traditional publishing deals, and $5,000-$20,000 increases in keynote speaking fees.

Academic Recognition & Professional Validation

Richard's practical expertise has earned academic recognition rarely achieved by non-academic practitioners. Professor Richard Makadok at Purdue University's Krannert School of Management adopted Richard's "How to Manage a Consulting Project" as required reading, providing this testimonial: "Great textbook for any college course that includes a field-study project for a client. Last year, this book helped my students to avoid many subtle pitfalls." Richard has served as a guest speaker for Purdue's entrepreneurship courses for four years, with students consistently rating his sessions as the "highlight of the semester."

Media Platform & Industry Authority

Richard's expertise is regularly featured across major media platforms, with 55+ podcast appearances including The Chris Voss Show, which reaches over one million listeners. He also hosts "Leaders and Their Stories," with nearly 100 episodes featuring tech founders, executives, and changemakers. His accelerating media presence (15 appearances in just two months during early 2025) demonstrates increasing industry demand for his insights.

Multi-Domain Creative Excellence

Beyond business expertise, Richard maintains an impressive creative portfolio with 950,000+ professional photographs documented across specialized events like Renaissance faires, masquerade balls, and entertainment industry functions. He served as court photographer for Southern California's belly dance community and has collaborated on creative projects like a science fiction novel with a platinum-selling rock star.

Emergency Response & Real-World Experience

Richard holds multiple CERT (Community Emergency Response Team) certifications and has survived extraordinary real-world disasters: three earthquakes over 7.1 magnitude, four hurricanes (including Category 4 Hurricane Milton in 2024), and a forest fire where his vehicle was surrounded by flames. This combination of official training and lived experience informs his emergency preparedness expertise and demonstrates resilience under extreme pressure.

Professional Ethics & Industry Leadership

Richard maintains industry-leading ethical standards through his publicly available Code of Ethics, which exceeds typical industry requirements and demonstrates transparency rarely seen in professional services. His business practices emphasize client protection, intellectual property safeguards, and honest service promotion, earning him a perfect 5.0/5 client rating and 96% satisfaction rate across all projects.

The Unique Value Proposition

What sets Richard apart is his ability to synthesize technical expertise, business leadership, creative skills, and ethical standards into solutions that single-specialty experts cannot provide. As he puts it: "Most ghostwriters come from journalism or English lit backgrounds. They're excellent writers, but they speak fluent liberal arts. I speak fluent nerd." This combination enables him to serve clients across industries (from biotech to technology to traditional business) while maintaining the storytelling excellence that transforms careers and secures millions in funding.

Richard's comprehensive professional background, validated through academic adoption, industry recognition, and measurable client outcomes, represents authentic expertise built through decades of real-world application rather than promotional claims. His approach combines systems thinking from technology leadership, visual storytelling from professional photography, and ethical standards that separate genuine expertise from manufactured credentials.

For leaders ready to transform their expertise into powerful narratives that build legacy, credibility, and business results, Richard Lowe brings the rare combination of technical knowledge, creative excellence, and proven business impact that makes the difference between a book and a breakthrough.

Books by Richard Lowe

See books by Richard Lowe at

https://masterofworlds.com

Get free publishing insights and industry updates at

https://thewritingking.substack.com

For ghostwriting and book coaching services see

https://thewritingking.com

www.ingramcontent.com/pod-product-compliance
Lightning Source LLC
Chambersburg PA
CBHW030934060726
47591CB00005B/1800